# WORLD ATLAS of THE PAST

# THE

# AGE OF DISCOVERY

# World Atlas

*of*

# The Past

3

*John Haywood*

# The

# Age of Discovery

Oxford University Press
New York

Published in the United States of America by
Oxford University Press, Inc.,
198 Madison Avenue
New York, NY 10016

Oxford is a registered trademark of Oxford University Press

ISBN 0-19-521691-1
ISBN 13: 978-0-19-521691-2

Library of Congress Cataloging-in-Publication Data available

*Academic consultant*
**Professor Jeremy Black**
University of Exeter, UK

*Project editor* Susan Kennedy
*Cartographic manager* Richard Watts
*Art editor* Ayala Kingsley

*Editors* Lauren Bourque, Peter Lewis
*Cartographic editor* Tim Williams
*Designer* Frankie Wood
*Picture researchers* Ayala Kingsley, Linda Proud
*Picture management* Claire Turner
*Production director* Clive Sparling
*Proofreader* Lynne Wycherley
*Indexer* Ann Barrett

The Brown Reference Group plc
(incorporating Andromeda Oxford Ltd)
8 Chapel Place
Rivington Street
London EC2A 3DQ

© 2004 The Brown Reference Group plc

Printed in China

# CONTENTS

# USING THIS ATLAS

This is the third of a four-volume set that charts the global story of humans from prehistoric times to the present day. The others are: THE ANCIENT WORLD (1), THE MEDIEVAL WORLD (2), and MODERN TIMES (4). Three different types of map are used in the World Atlas of the Past. Here are some hints on how to study the information that appears on them.

WORLD MAPS show what the world was like at a particular moment in human history. They will tell you where there were organized states and civilizations, where people lived mostly as farmers or pastoral nomads, and where they were predominantly hunter–gatherers. By following these maps through all four volumes of the Atlas you can see how human society has evolved over time and trace the rise and fall of political empires. Black-circled numbers on the world maps will help you locate references on the Timeline below.

REGIONAL MAPS show the history of a particular region of the world over an extended period of time (indicated in the top right corner of the page). To help you locate historic places, modern countries and borders are shown in light gray. Hill shading is included to indicate the physical landscape.

SUPPLEMENTARY MAPS add to the information in the regional maps by illustrating a particular theme or event.

The world and regional maps have grid references (numbers running vertically down the page, letters running horizontally across it). If you want to see if a particular place is shown on a map, the index will give you the page number and grid reference (eg. 37 4D) to help you locate it.

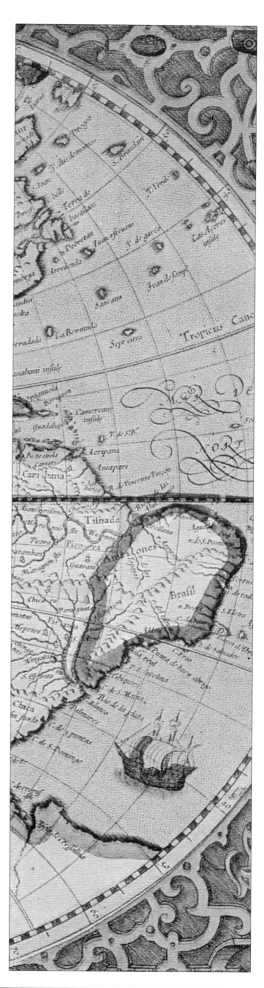

## STANDARD MAP INFORMATION

### World maps

| | |
|---|---|
| PERSIA | civilization, state, or empire |
| Dutch Guiana | chiefdom, dependency, or territory |
| *Khoisan herders* | tribe, people, or cultural group |

### Regional maps

| | |
|---|---|
| FRANCE | state or empire |
| Henan | dependency, territory, or province |
| *Goths* | tribe, people, or chiefdom |
| ANATOLIA | geographical region |
| LATVIA | modern country |
| ‒ ‒ ‒ | border of modern country |
| ✕ | battle |
| • | site, settlement, or town |

# INTRODUCTION

In the three centuries from 1492 to 1815 the world became a smaller place. European navigators and explorers charted the world's oceans and coastlines; by the end of the period all the continents, and most of the major island groups, had been written on to the maps. The period also saw a great shift in global power.

Before the Spanish set foot in the New World, Europe had been overshadowed by the more advanced civilizations of the Middle East and East Asia, who dominated international trade. The quantities of American gold and silver sent back to Europe brought a ready stream of wealth, and the opening of a direct sea route meant that European traders could buy silk and spices directly from Southeast Asia and the Far East. By the end of the 18th century Europeans controlled most of Asia's maritime trade. More shameful was the inhuman trade in slaves they had established between Africa and the Caribbean.

Europe itself underwent great religious and social upheavals between 1492 and 1815. It was split into opposing Catholic and Protestant camps by the Reformation and subsequently divided by frequent political wars, caused in part by rivalry for colonial trade. The French Revolution of 1789 threw Europe into turmoil. Napoleon emerged from the political chaos in France to make himself emperor, but his attempt to create an empire in Europe ended in his defeat in 1815. The French revolutionaries shared many of the ideals of liberty and democracy that inspired the thirteen American colonies to throw off British rule in 1776. By 1815, the young United States had established itself territorially and politically. The colonial empires of Latin America were also moving toward independence.

For all its success, Europe did not dominate the world in 1815. Most people in Asia, Africa, and the Pacific region had never seen or heard of Europeans. The largest empire was China, which controlled many neighboring states in Central and East Asia and had, like Japan, turned its back on contact with Europe. Closer to home, the Ottoman empire was still a challenge to European power, though it was obviously in decline. But western technological and scientific knowledge had seen rapid advances, and large-scale industrial production was just beginning in Britain. The global economy was set to grow as industrialization spread to the rest of Europe and the United States in the coming century.

*Left  Seventeenth-century Flemish still-life.*

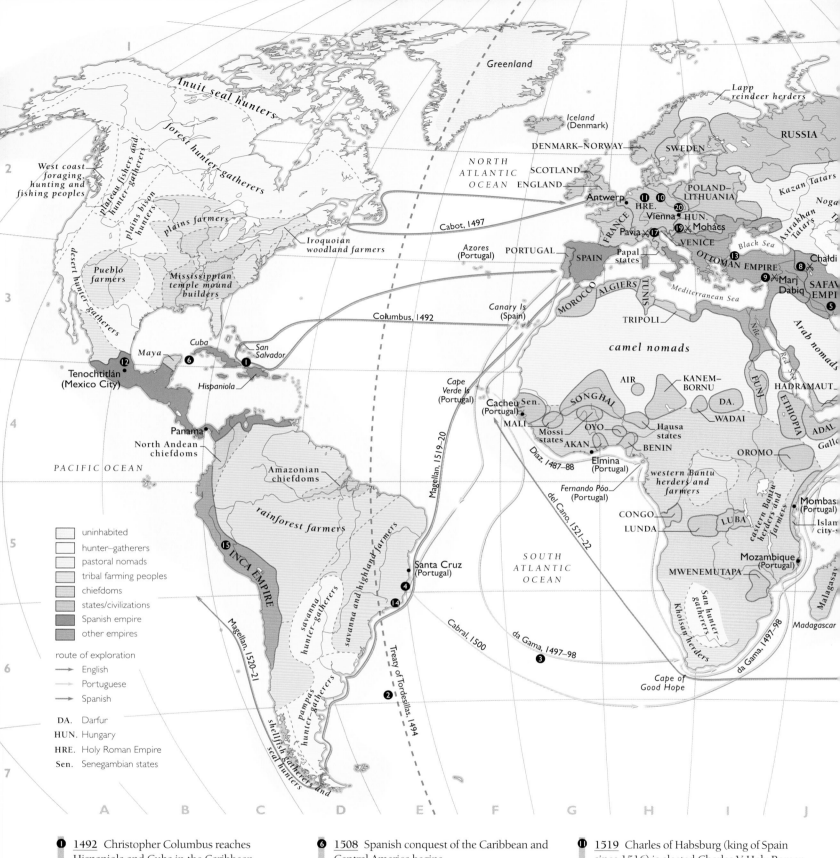

Greenland

*Inuit seal hunters*

*forest hunter-gatherers*

West coast
foraging,
hunting and
fishing peoples

*plateau fishers and*
*hunter-gatherers*

*plains bison*
*hunters*

*plains farmers*

desert hunter-gatherers

Pueblo
farmers

Mississippian
temple mound
builders

Iroquoian
woodland farmers

Cabot, 1497

NORTH
ATLANTIC
OCEAN

Iceland
(Denmark)

DENMARK–NORWAY

SWEDEN

*Lapp*
*reindeer herders*

RUSSIA

SCOTLAND

ENGLAND

Antwerp

**11** **10**

HRE.

Vienna

**20** HUN.

Mohács

**19**

POLAND-
LITHUANIA

Kazan Tatars

Noga

Astrakhan
Tatars

FRANCE

Pavia **17**

VENICE

OTTOMAN EMPIRE **13**

Chaldi

**8**

**9** Marj
Dabiq

SAFAV
EMPI

**5**

Azores
(Portugal)

PORTUGAL

SPAIN

Papal
states

Black Sea

Cuba

Maya

**6**

San Salvador

**1**

Columbus, 1492

Canary Is
(Spain)

MOROCCO ALGIERS

TUNIS

TRIPOLI

Mediterranean Sea

Nile

Red Sea

Arab nomads

**12**

Tenochtitlán
(Mexico City)

Hispaniola

*camel nomads*

Cape
Verde Is
(Portugal)

AIR

KANEM-
BORNU

DA.

WADAI

HADRAMAUT

ETHIOPIA

ADAL

Gallo

Panama

North Andean
chiefdoms

PACIFIC OCEAN

Amazonian
chiefdoms

*rainforest farmers*

Magellan, 1519–20

Diaz, 1487–88

Cacheu Sen.
(Portugal)

MALI

SONGHAI

Mossi
states

AKAN

OYO

Elmina
(Portugal)

BENIN

Hausa
states

*western Bantu*
*herders and*
*farmers*

Fernando Póo
(Portugal)

OROMO

CONGO

LUNDA

LUBA

*eastern Bantu*
*herders and*
*farmers*

Mombas
(Portugal)

Islam
city-

**15** INCA EMPIRE

*savanna*
*hunter-gatherers*

*savanna and highland farmers*

Santa Cruz
(Portugal)

**4**

**14**

del Cano, 1521–22

SOUTH
ATLANTIC
OCEAN

Mozambique
(Portugal)

MWENEMUTAPA

*San hunter-*
*gatherers*
*Khoisan herders*

Madagascar

*pampas*
*hunter-gatherers*

Magellan, 1520–21

Treaty of Tordesillas, 1494

Cabral, 1500

da Gama, 1497–98

**3**

da Gama, 1497–98

Cape of
Good Hope

*shellfish gatherers and*
*seal hunters*

uninhabited
hunter–gatherers
pastoral nomads
tribal farming peoples
chiefdoms
states/civilizations
Spanish empire
other empires

route of exploration

→ English
→ Portuguese
→ Spanish

DA.   Darfur
HUN.  Hungary
HRE.  Holy Roman Empire
Sen.  Senegambian states

A   B   C   D   E   F   G   H   I   J

**1** **1492** Christopher Columbus reaches
Hispaniola and Cuba in the Caribbean

**2** **1494** The Treaty of Tordesillas gives all land
west of an imaginary line in the Atlantic to
Spain, and all land east of it to Portugal

**3** **1497–98** Vasco da Gama makes the first
return voyage from Portugal to India

**4** **1500** Pedro Alvarez Cabral discovers Brazil for
Portugal, while sailing to India

**5** **1501** The Safavid dynasty is set up in Persia

**6** **1508** Spanish conquest of the Caribbean and
Central America begins

**7** **1511** The Portuguese capture Malacca

**8** **1514** The Ottoman Turks defeat the Safavids at
the battle of Chaldiran

**9** **1516** The Ottoman Turks defeat the Mamluke
rulers of Egypt at the battle of Marj Dabiq

**10** **1517** Martin Luther publishes his 95 Theses in
Wittenberg, Germany, an act that leads to the
Protestant Reformation

**11** **1519** Charles of Habsburg (king of Spain
since 1516) is elected Charles V, Holy Roman
emperor, on the death of his grandfather

**12** **1519** The Spanish adventurer Hernán Cortés
begins the conquest of the Aztec empire

**13** **1520** Suleiman I becomes the reigning sultan
of the Ottoman empire

**14** **1521** The Portuguese begin to colonize Brazil

**15** **1521–25** The Inca empire in Peru reaches its
greatest extent

Map labels (left side):

Inuit seal hunters
Siberian hunter-gatherers
Siberian reindeer herders
ir Tatars
Ainu hunter-gatherers
Central Asian khanates
Mongols
Kirghiz
Kalmyks
egs
Beijing
KOREA JAPAN
Kabul
MUGHAL EMPIRE
TIBET
MING CHINESE EMPIRE
Nanjing
Panipat
⑱
Islamic and Hindu states
Shan states
OMAN
BENGAL
Burmese kingdoms
GHARRA
Taiwan
LAOS
AHRA
ORISSA
MEN
Goa (Portugal)
PEGU
ANNAM
Philippine Is
VIJAYANAGARA
AYUTTHAYA
ama, 1497–98
SAYLAN
Ceylon
CAMBODIA
Cabral, 1500
Colombo (Portugal)
Lopez de Sequeira, 1509–10
Perestrello, 1514–16
⑦
Magellan 1520–21
del Cano, 1521
Malacca (Portugal)
MALACCA
Borneo
New Guinea
Sumatra
Malaysian Islamic states
Papuan farmers
Java
Timor (Portugal)
Melanesians
INDIAN OCEAN
Australian Aboriginal hunter-gatherers
del Cano, 1521–22
⑯
Polynesians
Tasmanian hunter-gatherers
Maori chiefdoms

L M N O P

# THE WORLD BY 1530

IN THE LATE 15TH CENTURY, THE WORLD'S GREATEST CIVILIZATIONS WERE ALL IN ASIA; EUROPE WAS BACKWARD BY COMPARISON. YET BY 1530 EUROPEANS CONTROLLED THE INDIAN OCEAN, AND WERE ON THE WAY TO CONQUERING THE GREAT EMPIRES OF THE AMERICAS. ONE SHIP, COMMANDED BY FERDINAND MAGELLAN, HAD SAILED AROUND THE WORLD. THE IMPLICATIONS FOR WORLD HISTORY WERE ENORMOUS.

Trade in the rich cloths, jewels, and spices of Asia was the chief goal of the European explorers. Such luxury goods had great value in Europe. However, western traders did not have direct access to the profitable markets of Asia—their way was blocked by hostile Muslim states such as the Ottoman Turks who by 1530 controlled the Black Sea and eastern Mediterranean ports at the western end of the overland route from China and India, as well as the sea route from the Indian Ocean to the Red Sea and Egypt.

During the 15th century, European navigators had begun looking for other routes to Asia. They were led by the Portuguese who learned to build ships that were capable of making the long sea voyage down the Atlantic coast of Africa; in 1497–98 Vasco da Gama sailed from Portugal to India and back around the Cape of Good Hope. More daring still, in 1492 Christopher Columbus ventured west across the Atlantic with a Spanish fleet in an attempt to reach China. But instead of arriving in Asia, he had found

*Right The "Santa Maria," flagship of the small fleet with which Columbus sailed in 1492, resembled this tiny vessel. The crossing from the Canary Islands to landfall at San Salvador (Bahamas) took almost six weeks.*

⑯ 1522 Magellan's voyage around the world (begun in 1519) is completed by Sebastian del Cano

⑰ 1525 Francis I of France is captured by the Spanish at the battle of Pavia in northern Italy

⑱ 1526 Babur defeats the sultan of Delhi at the battle of Panipat and conquers northern India

⑲ 1526 An Ottoman army defeats the Hungarians at Mohács

⑳ 1529 The Ottomans besiege Vienna

the way to a new continent, soon to be called America. Other explorers followed and a few years later John Cabot sailed from England to Newfoundland. In 1520 Ferdinand Magellan entered the Pacific Ocean around the tip of South America. Although he died en route, his crew returned to Europe having made the first circumnavigation of the globe.

## EUROPE

By 1530 Spain was the wealthiest kingdom in Europe, profiting from the gold that the Spanish conquerors discovered in the Americas and shipped home in vast quantities. In 1519 the Spanish king became, as Charles V, the Holy Roman emperor. This gave him control of Spain, Germany, the Netherlands, and much of Italy, and created a Habsburg power bloc that would dominate Europe for 200 years. Spain's only political rival was France. Since the start of the century they had been fighting a long war for control of the rich city-states of northern Italy. By 1530 it was clear that Spain would be the eventual winner.

The greatest event in Europe in the first half of the 16th century was the controversy over religious reform. Many Christians felt that the Catholic church, and the popes in particular, had become corrupt. In 1517, a German monk, Martin Luther, launched a movement of protest against church abuses. It fueled religious and political unrest in Germany and led to the Protestant Reformation, which divided Europe into bitterly opposed camps for 150 years. By 1530 the Reformation had spread to Sweden, and would soon reach England and Scotland.

## THE MIDDLE EAST

In 1530 the Ottoman Turks dominated the Middle East. They had begun to expand out of Anatolia (mainland Turkey) into the Balkans in the 13th and 14th centuries; the city of Constantinople (Istanbul) was taken in 1453. In 1514 they seized Mesopotamia (modern Iraq) from the Safavid rulers of Persia, and the invasion of Egypt two years later laid the way open for further expansion in North Africa and Arabia. The Ottomans continued, too, to make inroads into Europe. After the Hungarians were defeated in 1526, an Ottoman army reached Vienna,

one of the leading cities of Europe and the seat of the Habsburg emperors, in 1529. It failed to capture the city, but few believed the threat to Europe was over. In 1530 the sultan Suleiman I ("the Magnificent") was the most powerful man in the world.

## AFRICA

Before the European discovery of America, tropical west Africa had been the main source of gold for Europe and the Middle East. Caravans of camels conveyed it across the Sahara desert to ports on the North African coast. This trans-Saharan trade was controlled by the kingdom of Songhai, but when the Portuguese set up a string of bases on the west African coast in the late 15th century, they took trade away from the Saharan routes, thus weakening Songhai. Defeat by the neighboring state of Hausa in 1517 hastened its decline.

Portuguese traders were steadily developing their activities in Africa. By 1502 they were sending African slaves to the Americas. They used their warships to attack the

*Left* *A Venetian ambassador is received by the Ottomans, in a painting by Giovanni Bellini. Venice had once been the most powerful naval and trading power in the Mediterranean, but its days were numbered. The Ottomans had taken over many of its island fortresses, and with the opening up of the new ocean-going trade routes, Antwerp replaced it as the main European market for the spice trade.*

Mongols. The Ming rulers were resistant to outside influences and foreign trade, and as a result, China had begun to lose its technological lead over the rest of the world.

In Central Asia, the growing power of the Ottomans and the Russians was beginning to push the nomadic tribes of the steppes eastward after several centuries of movement in the opposite direction. One nomadic tribal leader, Babur, captured Kabul in Afghanistan in 1504 and went on to invade India. He defeated the sultan of Delhi in 1526 and founded the Mughal dynasty that ruled much of India until the 18th century.

In 1510 the Portuguese founded a trading base at Goa in India. The following year they seized the important Malayan port of Malacca, thereby laying the foundations for what would become a powerful trading empire in the East Indies.

## THE AMERICAS

European impact in Central and South America had disastrous consequences for the indigenous peoples. The colonists and adventurers who followed Columbus west were greedy for gold and wasted little time in plundering the wealth of the Aztec empire in Mexico. Virtually all of Central America had been conquered by 1530, and Francisco Pizarro was preparing to invade the Inca empire from the Spanish colony in Panama. By 1533 it, too, would have fallen to the conquistadors.

*Below* *This silver alpaca was made as a ritual offering by the Incas. South America had vast natural and mineral wealth before the arrival of the Europeans. Herds of alpacas – which gave thick, soft wool – and llamas, providing food, power, cloth and hides, made the steep Andean mountainsides productive. Peru's vast reserves of gold and silver proved irresistible to European explorers.*

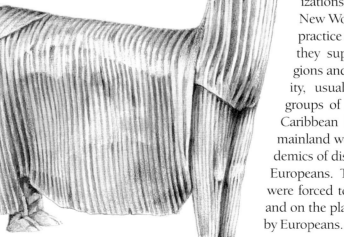

The Spanish showed little or no interest in the civilizations they found in the New World. Horrified by the practice of human sacrifice, they suppressed native religions and imposed Christianity, usually by force. Entire groups of Amerindians in the Caribbean islands and on the mainland were destroyed in epidemics of diseases introduced by Europeans. Those who survived were forced to work in the mines and on the plantations established by Europeans.

Arab traders who had controlled trade in the Indian Ocean for centuries, and Muslim trading ports on the east African coast were brought under their influence. The Portuguese also helped the Christian kingdom of Ethiopia defeat its Muslim neighbor, Adal.

## SOUTH & EAST ASIA

China was the world's largest state in the 16th century. Since 1368 it had been ruled by the Ming dynasty, which had come to power after a century of devastation by the

# THE SPANISH–AMERICAN EMPIRE

IN 1492, THE ITALIAN-BORN NAVIGATOR CHRISTOPHER COLUMBUS SAILED WEST ACROSS THE ATLANTIC IN SEARCH OF A SEA ROUTE TO CHINA. SPONSORED BY THE CATHOLIC MONARCHS, FERDINAND AND ISABELLA, HE SAILED UNDER THE FLAG OF SPAIN. HE MADE LANDFALL ON AN ISLAND IN THE CARIBBEAN, THE FIRST EUROPEAN CONTACT WITH THE AMERICAS SINCE THE VIKINGS. AS WORD OF COLUMBUS'S DISCOVERIES IN THE "NEW WORLD" SPREAD, OTHER EUROPEAN EXPLORERS FOLLOWED IN HIS FOOTSTEPS.

Columbus made four journeys across the Atlantic to the Caribbean. He claimed all the islands he visited for Spain and founded a settlement on Hispaniola. In 1499 a Spanish fleet explored along the coast of South America. One ship was captained by a certain Amerigo Vespucci; an early map-maker ascribed his forename (Americus in Latin) to the new continents, and they have been known as the Americas ever since.

The New World held out unparalleled opportunities for personal enrichment and national conquest. Spanish military adventurers, known as conquistadors, followed on the heels of the early explorers. Rumors of the vast wealth possessed by the Aztec rulers of Mexico led the conquistador Hernán Cortés, at the head of an army of only a few hundred, to invade and conquer their empire in 1519–24. An even smaller force under the command of Francisco Pizarro overcame the far larger Inca empire of the Andes in 1531–35. Huge quantities of gold and silver were plundered from both empires and shipped back to Europe. Stories of a fabulously rich city, El Dorado ("The Golden"), buried deep in the jungle, traveled back with the treasure ships. Many expeditions were sent to look for it, but they all failed. Instead, the conquistadors met with disease, starvation, and the poisoned arrows of hostile Amerindians. But their quest resulted in large areas of the Americas being explored and mapped by Europeans.

## THE IMPACT OF CONQUEST

As a result of the Spanish presence, the indigenous New World peoples suffered a huge loss of life. More died in epidemics than in war—the native Amerindian population lacked immunity to European diseases such as smallpox. The Carib and Arawak peoples of the Caribbean, who were treated with extreme harshness, were nearly extinct by 1550, while the numbers of Aztecs, Incas, and other South American peoples had more than halved by 1600 and continued to decline throughout the next 100 years. The Spanish imported African slaves to make up for the loss of workers on the sugar plantations they established in the Caribbean. The Amerindians of Central and South America were forced to work in the rich silver mines of Mexico and Peru.

The Spanish believed they had a divine duty to convert the Amerindians to Christianity. They refused to tolerate pagan worship; in banning it, they suppressed many aspects of native culture. Dominican and Franciscan friars set up schools where European farming methods and crafts were taught. Though harshly run, they offered some protection against the cruelty of the conquistadors. Later, the Jesuits founded

*Above* A Dominican friar supervises an Inca woman at her loom.

Map legend:
- Portuguese territory, 1650
- Portuguese territory, 1750
- Spanish territory, 1650
- Spanish territory, 1750
- Jesuit mission state to 1767
- British territory, 1750
- Dutch territory, 1750
- French territory, 1750

early settlement or trading post, with date of foundation
- Portuguese
- Spanish
- archbishopric
- line of Treaty of Tordesillas, 1494
- route of explorer
- route of conquistador
- slaving expedition of the Paulistas
- circumnavigation by Francis Drake, 1577–80

0 — 1400 km
0 — 1000 mi

NORTH
ATLANTIC
OCEAN

Bermuda Islands
to Britain

Columbus, 1492

St Augustine
1565
Florida
New
Orleans
Ponce de Leon, 1512–13
Columbus, 1493
Lesser Antilles
Bahamas
San Juan
1511
Puerto
Rico
Columbus, 1498
Matanzas
Havana
1515
Cuba
Hispaniola
Santo Domingo
1496
Vespucci 1499
Gulf of
Mexico
..., 1519
Jamaica

Columbus, 1502-4
Cumaná
1521
Paramaribo
Cayenne
Ceará
Caracas
1567
Georgetown
Guiana
Highlands
São Luis do
Maranhão
1615
Natal
1597
Olinda
1537
Cartagena
1533
Bele
do Para
1616
Recife
1563
PACIFIC
OCEAN
Antigua
1542
Guatemala
Porto Bello
1597
Nombre de Dios
1510
VENEZUELA
Orinoco
Amazon
Portuguese
Spanish
Panama
1519
Pizarro, 1526-27
Santa Fe de Bogota
1538
COLOMBIA
Negro
Manaus
1674
Tocantins
São Francisco
Bahia
1549
Quito
1534
BRAZIL
Santa Cruz
Guayaquil
1535
Japura
Amazon
Basin
Putumayo
Xingu
Tapajós
Brazilian
Highlands
Juruá
Purus
Madeira
Ucayali
Mato
Grosso
Plateau
Villa Rica
1698
ANDES
Pizarro, 1533
PERU
Rio de Janeiro
1565
São Paulo
1532
SãoVicente
1530
Cuzco
BOLIVIA
Callao
1537
Ciudad de los Reyes
(Lima)
1535
La Paz
Chuquisaca
(Charcas/La Plata)
1538
Paraguay
Paraná
PARAGUAY
Arica
1537
Potosí
Asunción
1538
ANDES
Banda
Oriental
Córdoba
1573
Buenos
Aires
1536
ARGENTINA
Valparaiso
1541
Santiago
1541
SOUTH
ATLANTIC
OCEAN
Valdivia
1552
Patagonia
Spanish
Portuguese

mission states in the frontier regions. Spanish gradually replaced native languages.

The whole of Central America was made the Viceroyalty of New Spain. Another viceroyalty was established in Peru shortly after Pizarro's conquest. Both viceroyalties expanded as settlements were founded in California, Texas, and Florida, and east of the Andes, and were later divided into smaller administrative regions.

*Above* African slaves were sent in large numbers to the New World. This heavily armed "mulatto," the term used for people of mixed African and European descent, was painted by a visitor to Brazil in the 1630s.

*Above* Colonial life in Brazil and Spanish America reproduced the patterns of life at home. Towns were built in European architectural styles to serve the local neighborhood. In this 17th-century Brazilian town, the main square is the site of the slave market: plantation owners stroll up and down to inspect the most recent consignments. The slave trade was made illegal in the Spanish colonies by the 1820s, but continued in the coffee plantations of Brazil until the late 19th century.

The conquistadors were given parcels of land called *encomienda*. Each *encomendero* (lord) was entitled to collect taxes and use local labor in return for keeping soldiers to defend the empire, in much the same way as the Aztecs and Incas had maintained their empires. In time, the Spanish created large farming estates (*haciendas*). Colonists were always in short supply, the more so as emigration from Spain was restricted in the 17th century to a limit of 2,000 a year to stem falling population levels at home. The Spanish in South America became absentee landlords, staying in the towns, or returning to Europe, for long periods. Amerindians were made to leave the land to become wage laborers, or peons, on the *haciendas*. This system remains in force in many parts of Central and South America.

## EUROPEAN RIVALS

Its American empire turned Spain into the greatest power in Europe. The silver that was shipped back in huge quantities helped to finance its wars, and the flow of precious metal stimulated the whole European economy. Other European countries were eager to grab a share of the New World's riches. The Treaty of Tordesillas between Spain and

### END OF THE SPANISH & PORTUGUESE EMPIRES

UNITED STATES OF AMERICA

MEXICO
1821

ATLANTIC OCEAN

Cuba

HAITI
1804

Jamaica

Puerto Rico

Mosquito Coast

British Honduras
UNITED PROVINCES OF
CENTRAL AMERICA
(1821–23 to Mexico)
1823

British Guiana
Dutch Guiana
French Guiana

REPUBLIC OF GRAN COLOMBIA
1819

BRAZIL
1822

PACIFIC OCEAN

PERU
1821

BOLIVIA
1825

PARAGUAY
1811

CHILE
1818

ARGENTINE CONFEDERATION
(United Provinces of La Plata, 1816–25)
1816

Patagonia

Malvinas
(Falklands)

Portuguese territory, early 19th century

Spanish territory, early 19th century

remaining Spanish territory in the Americas, 1825

borders, 1825

**1818** date of independence

Portugal in 1494 had drawn an imaginary line to bisect the Atlantic west of the Cape Verde islands: the Portuguese were free to settle all land to the east of it, the Spanish all land to the west. In effect, this restricted the Portuguese to a small area of coastal Brazil, which they began to settle in large numbers in the 1530s. Portuguese slavers, known as *Paulistas*, frequently raided into the Brazilian jungle, where they attacked the Spanish Jesuit mission states. In the late 17th century, to avoid war with Spain, Portugal cracked down on such raids, banning the enslavement of Native Americans. To provide labor in their mines and plantations they imported black slaves from Angola on the west coast of Africa.

For a long time, other European countries such as the Netherlands, England, and France had to confine their activities in the New World to attacking Spain's ships and coastal ports. Piracy and smuggling were common; so too was privateering, in which the captain of a commercial ship was authorized to carry out piracy on behalf of a hostile government. The English privateer Sir Francis Drake was particularly famous for his daring raids around the Caribbean. But even he failed to capture the heavily guarded treasure fleet that carried quantities of recently mined American silver back to Spain every year. It was seized only once, by the Dutch admiral Piet Heyn in 1628.

# SPANISH DECLINE

In the 17th century, the Spanish-American economy collapsed, partly through labor shortages caused by the dramatic fall in the Amerindian population. The Netherlands, England, and France seized advantage of Spain's weakness to set up small colonies of their own in Central and South America: the English capture of Jamaica in 1655 was a particularly expensive loss. Spanish territory in North America was also threatened by the success of French and English colonies (see pages 16–19). At the conclusion of the Seven Years War (1756–63) Britain exchanged Havana (captured in 1762) for Florida, but had lost it again by 1783.

In spite of these losses, the Spanish and Portuguese American empires were mostly intact at the end of the 18th century. However, independence movements were starting to develop, fueled partly by the ideals of the American and French Revolutions. The Napoleonic wars in Europe, when Spain and Portugal were under French occupation (see pages 28–31), provided the catalyst for revolt. The battle for independence started in Mexico in 1810. In 1811 Simón Bolívar (the "Liberator"), an inspired military leader, began the struggle to free South America from Spanish rule. Within 15 years the Spanish empire had broken up, and Brazil was also independent.

# THE CATHOLIC LEGACY

*Although it was imposed by force, Roman Catholicism put down deep roots among the native peoples of Latin America. Today, half the world's Catholics live there. Many traditional beliefs and customs were assimilated into Catholicism, giving it a distinctive Amerindian character. In the Andes, sacrifices were made to Christian saints to placate the mountain gods. The figure of Christ was associated with the Sun-god and the Virgin Mary with Mama Cocha, the Inca earth-goddess. In Mexico, belief in the sacredness of ancestors remains alive in the vivid celebrations on the Day of the Dead (November 1st), the Christian remembrance of All Souls.*

*Right Guatemalan villagers celebrate the feast of St. Thomas by carrying his statue through the streets.*

# COLONIAL NORTH AMERICA

IN 1500 NORTH AMERICA WAS INHABITED BY SCATTERED GROUPS OF NATIVE AMERICAN FARMERS AND HUNTER–GATHERERS. THE FIRST EUROPEANS WHO CAME HERE HAD NO IDEA OF THE CONTINENT'S TRUE SIZE AND DIVERSITY, AND FOUND IT AN ALIEN, ENIGMATIC PLACE. SATISFIED THAT IT HELD NO RESERVES OF GOLD OR SILVER, SPAIN MADE LITTLE ATTEMPT TO COLONIZE IT, AND IT WAS LEFT FOR THE NORTHERN EUROPEAN NATIONS TO DO SO.

In 1497, John Cabot, an Italian-born seafarer sailing under the English flag, set out from Bristol across the Atlantic in the hope of finding a northern sea route to China. He reached Newfoundland, becoming the first European to arrive in North America since the Vikings had made a temporary camp there 500 years earlier. He found the waters were teeming with cod, and English fishing fleets visited the island regularly thereafter, but no permanent settlement was established there until 1610.

Giovanni da Verrazano sailed the length of the Atlantic seaboard in 1524, and the French sailor, Jacques Cartier, explored the St. Lawrence river in 1535–36, searching for a way through the heart of the northern continent; others tried to sail around it. The sheer scale of North America was beyond any European's ability to imagine.

Early visitors reported that it was covered in forest and inhabited by hostile peoples. The first attempts at colonization ended in failure. Eventually, in 1607, an English settlement took root at Jamestown, Virginia. Quebec was founded a year later by the French, and by 1650 there was a scattering of colonies along the eastern seaboard, Swedish and Dutch among them.

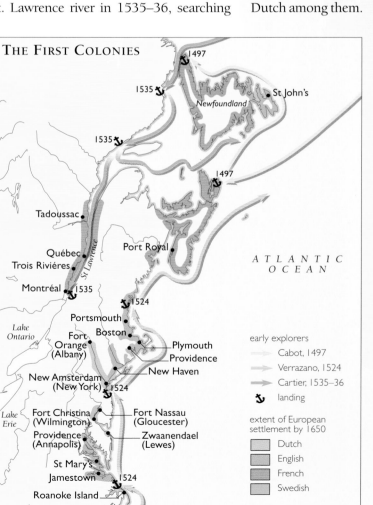

## THE FIRST COLONIES

Newfoundland

St John's

ATLANTIC OCEAN

Tadoussac
Québec
Trois Riviéres
Port Royal
Montréal 1535
Lake Ontario
Portsmouth
Fort Orange (Albany)
Boston
Plymouth
Providence
New Haven
New Amsterdam (New York) 1524
Lake Erie
Fort Christina (Wilmington)
Fort Nassau (Gloucester)
Providence (Annapolis)
Zwaanendael (Lewes)
St Mary's
Jamestown 1524
Roanoke Island

early explorers
— Cabot, 1497
→ Verrazano, 1524
→ Cartier, 1535–36
⚓ landing

extent of European settlement by 1650
Dutch
English
French
Swedish

*Above* The artist John White took part in several expeditions to North America and for a time was governor of Sir Walter Raleigh's shortlived colony on Roanoke Island (1587). His paintings are among the earliest pictures of Native American society. The "towne of Pomeiock" depicts a stockaded village of bark longhouses.

## TRADE & COEXISTENCE

The first French settlers in North America were fur trappers. They were soon trading with the local people, exchanging firearms, iron implements, and brandy for animal skins. There was a huge European demand for North American furs; beavers, in particular, were highly valued by the hat trade. French explorers made their way down the St. Lawrence, discovering the Great Lakes. They traveled into the interior, and followed the Mississippi river to the Gulf of Mexico.

The French aside, colonists from north Europe tended to be farmers, who cleared the forests to exploit the rich farmlands of the Atlantic seaboard and quickly developed a European-style agricultural economy. The native peoples welcomed settlers

Lake Athabasca

Western Woods Cree

Chipewy

Saskatchewan

Plains Cree

Fort Le Pas
Fort Bourbon
Fort Dauphir

D  E  F  G  H  I  J  K

Coats
Island

Mansel
Island

*Inuit*

*Inuit*

*Naskapi*

H U D S O N
B A Y

*Eastern
Cree*

Belcher
Islands

*Montagnais*

Newfoundland

St John's

■ Fort Churchill

Port
Nelson ■ ■ Fort York

■ Fort Severn

*Ile Royale
(Cape Breton I)*

■ Louisbourg

*Rupert's Land*
(Hudson's Bay Company)

■ Fort Albany

Fort Rupert ■

Moose
Factory ■

Tadoussac ■

*Cree*

CANADA

*Lake
Winnipeg*

Québec ■

Ft Beausejour ■

*Nova Scotia*

Halifax ■

Port Royal ■

Trois Riviéres ■

*New France*

Montréal ■

*Iroquois*

Fort La
Tourette ■

*Ojibwa*

■ Fort
Népigon

New Hampshire

Fort Maurepas ■

*Huron*

Crown Point ■ Ticonderoga

Portsmouth

Fort La Reine ■

Fort St ■
Pierre

Fort St ■
Charles

Fort Michipicton ■

*Lake
Superior*

Fort ■
Kaministiquia

Sault St ■
Marie

Fort Frontenac ■

Fort
William
Henry ■

Fort
George ■

Boston ■

Massachusetts

Albany ■ Plymouth

Providence

*Gros
Ventre*

Fort
St Croix ■

*Lake Huron*

Fort Oswego ■

Fort ■
Ontario

New ■
York

New Haven ■

Connecticut

Fort Rouillé ■

*Lake Ontario*

New York City ■

*Mandan*

*Winnebago*

Fort Niagara ■

*Ottawa*

*Pennsylvania*

New Jersey

*Sioux*

*Mississippi*

Fort St Joseph ■

*Lake Michigan*

*Lake Erie*

Fort
Presqu'isle ■

*Delaware*

Philadelphia ■

ATLANTIC
OCEAN

Fort ■
Beauharnais

Fort
Pontchartrain ■

Delaware

Baltimore ■

Maryland

Fort St Louis ■

Fort Duquesne
(Fort Pitt) ■

Fort
Necessity ■

Annapolis ■

Fort Crevecoeur ■

*Miami  Wyandot*

Fort Pickawillany ■

Virginia

Richmond ■

Williamsburg ■

*Missouri*

*Shawnee*

Jamestown ■

*Tuscarora*

Fort ■
Vincennes

*Kaintuck*

North
Carolina

Fort Orléans ■

New Bern ■

UNITED STATES
OF AMERICA

Fort Chartres ■

*Cherokee*

*Chickasaw*

*A P P A L A C H I A N*

Wilmington ■

Fort Prudhomme ■

*Choctaw*

*Creek*

South
Carolina

Fort Augusta ■

Georgetown ■

Charleston ■

*M T S*

Fort King
George ■

Savannah ■

Georgia

Fort
Rosalie ■

*Louisiana*

*Alabama*

*Yamassee*

St Augustine ■

Fort
Condé ■

Pensacola ●

*Florida*

*Natchez*

New Orleans ■

*Gulf of
Mexico*

settlement or trading post
founded since 1650

■ British

■ French

extent of European settlement in 1713

British

French

Spanish

extent of European settlement, 1750

British

French

Spanish

French and Indian War, 1754–63

⚑ fort or settlement captured by the British

⚑ fort or settlement captured by the French

→ exploration by La Salle, 1681–82

colonial road

native American trade route

*Ute* native American peoples

0 ———————— 600 km

0 ———————— 400 mi

17

for the trade they brought, but prevented expansion inland; the Appalachian mountains also posed a formidable barrier. The first settlers in New England were mostly Puritans, strict Protestants who had left England to avoid religious persecution, and hoped to create a truly godly society in the New World. Hardworking people, many became prosperous through farming and commerce, and enjoyed a higher standard of living and higher life expectancy than most people in England.

The Virginian settlements of the south were mostly sponsored by English aristocrats as a form of investment. They hoped to establish plantations using the labor of servants, wage laborers, African slaves, and convicted criminals who had chosen emigration to America as an alternative to jail. Virginia's subtropical climate was unfamiliar to the first settlers, and many died from disease or starvation. The cultivation of tobacco, a native American plant, for export to Europe later made Virginia as wealthy as the New England trading ports.

## GROWING CONFLICTS

From the start, women and children had numbered among the colonists beginning new lives in North America. The European settlers on the eastern seaboard soon outnumbered the Native American peoples. As their towns and villages expanded, they took over new areas of land, making conflict inevitable. Relations between the settlers and Native Americans worsened in the course of the 17th century as attacks on European settlements grew. The colonists

responded by driving the Native Americans from their traditional territories. As in Spanish America, the native peoples lost huge numbers to mass epidemics of European diseases, reducing their relatively small and fragmented tribes still further.

Europe's wars often spilled over into the North American colonies, leading to armed skirmishes and warfare. New Sweden (Delaware) was captured by the Dutch in 1655, but they lost it to the English in 1664, along with their settlement of New Amsterdam, which became New York.

As English settlement began to extend inland to the St. Lawrence and Great Lakes, tensions built up with the French. From 1686, the French attacked English trading posts on Hudson Bay and, in alliance with the Huron Indians, raided New England. Rivalry was even stronger in the 18th century. In the French and Indian War (1754–63) the British used their navy to blockade France's colonies in North America. After the capture of Quebec (1759) and Montreal (1760) the British took control of all settlement east of the Mississippi river. More than 60,000 French settlers were left under British rule, but were allowed to continue living under French laws.

### POCAHONTAS

*Many legends surround the figure of Pocahontas, a Native American Powhatan who befriended the English settlers at Jamestown and is supposed to have intervened to spare the life of the colony's founder, John Smith. She was later baptized and married an Englishman, John Rolfe. This early portrait shows her in European dress during her stay in England in 1616. Advertised as an Indian princess, she became an instant celebrity, but died there of smallpox.*

**Left** *The labor of the early settlers transformed the New England landscape to give us the familiar vistas we see today. Forests were cleared and swamps drained for agriculture, creating a close patchwork of small farms and rural communities.*

**Below** *This 1710 print of an armed, tobacco-smoking frontiersman presents a typical image of Canadian life. French fur trappers relied on native guides and formed closer links with Native Americans than the English colonists did.*

## A DISTINCT SOCIETY

By 1775 the population of the 13 colonies of British North America was about 2.25 million, more than a quarter of Britain's. In Virginia, slave numbers had increased from 15,000 in 1700 to 190,000 by 1775, almost half the population. Owners, fearful of rebellion, treated them harshly.

The American colonists were still strongly influenced by British culture: the well-off liked to wear the latest London fashion. But there were growing differences. People were more self-reliant, and the lack of an aristocracy made it easier for all classes to succeed. There was no state church to impose uniformity of religion, as was the case in Britain. A large influx of Germans, Scots, and Irish settlers since the 1720s had radically altered the English character of some of the colonies. Along with an American dialect of English, a distinctly American society was emerging.

## TIMETABLE

**1497**
John Cabot is the first European to visit North America since the Vikings

**1535–36**
Jacques Cartier explores the St. Lawrence river

**1584–90**
Sir Walter Raleigh founds a settlement on Roanoke island, but it fails

**1607**
The first permanent English colony is established at Jamestown, Virginia

**1608**
Champlain, "founder of Canada," establishes a settlement at Quebec and explores Lake Champlain

**1620**
The Pilgrims, an extreme Puritan sect, land at Plymouth, Massachusetts

**1622**
Native Americans kill 350 colonists at Jamestown after their lands are taken

**1626**
The Dutch found New Amsterdam

**1636**
Harvard University is founded

**1664**
The English capture New Amsterdam and rename it New York

**1675–76**
King Philip's War is waged between Native Americans and colonists

**1681–82**
La Salle explores the Mississippi river

**1732**
Georgia is founded as the 13th British American colony

**1754–63**
The French and Indian War is fought

**1759**
The British defeat the French at the Plains of Abraham, leading to the capture of Quebec

**1763**
The British suffer initial defeats by the Native Americans in Pontiac's War

**1763**
The Treaty of Paris confirms British control of French America

# THE AMERICAN REVOLUTION

GREAT BRITAIN'S VICTORY OVER FRANCE IN 1763 MADE IT THE STRONGEST COLONIAL POWER IN THE WORLD. BUT WITHOUT THE IMMEDIATE THREAT OF FRENCH INVASION, THE THIRTEEN AMERICAN COLONIES HAD LESS REASON FOR REMAINING LOYAL TO BRITAIN. THE IMPOSITION OF TAXES AND RESTRICTIONS ON OVERSEAS TRADE LED TO INCREASING DISSATISFACTION WITH BRITISH RULE. IN 1776 THE THIRTEEN COLONIES DECLARED THEIR INDEPENDENCE FROM BRITAIN. WAR FOLLOWED, AND IN 1783 THE UNITED STATES OF AMERICA WAS BORN.

*Below* One of the most famous events in American history: a group of angry colonists, dressed as Native Americans, sneaked aboard a British ship and dumped its cargo of tea in Boston Harbor.

Most people in Britain believed that the main purpose of colonies was to further the interests of trade in the home country by supplying cheap raw materials for manufacturing and providing an export market for goods. During the 17th century laws were passed to prevent the American colonies from trading with countries other than Britain. This had the effect of creating a flourishing illegal trade with the Spanish, French, and Dutch colonies of the Caribbean. During the French and Indian War, merchants in New England began to export goods directly to Europe in their own ships, and once peace was signed the British government increased customs controls in an attempt to halt the trade. This caused great resentment. Plantation owners in the south were also afraid that Britain's increasing opposition to slavery would cause the collapse of their plantation economy .

Yet another cause of resentment was the Proclamation Line of 1763, which forbade colonial settlement west of the Appalachian mountains. The intention was to prevent clashes with the uprooted Native American groups forced inland from their traditional lands by European settlement. But the continued flow of immigrants and overcrowding of the coastal colonies meant that there was relentless pressure to keep pushing the frontier westward, and many colonists simply ignored the law.

## "NO TAXES!"

The war with France had been expensive, and the British government decided to raise money by taxing the colonists. The Stamp Act, introduced in 1765, imposed a tax on legal documents and newspapers. The colonists, who had never been directly taxed before, were outraged. British goods were boycotted and representatives of all 13 colonies met in a special congress to oppose the move. Taking as their slogan "No taxation without representation," they declared they would not pay the tax because they had no voice in the British Parliament.

The Stamp Act was quickly withdrawn but replaced almost immediately with taxes on tea, glass, lead, paint, and paper. Once again the government backed down in the face of boycotts, and all but the tea tax were withdrawn. Protests mounted and turned violent. In 1770 British soldiers shot dead five people during a riot in Boston, an event that came to be immortalized as the Boston Massacre and heightened popular feeling against the British still further.

In December 1773, the Boston Tea Party occurred. The British responded to this act of defiance by passing a series of punitive measures, called the Intolerable Acts. They united all the colonies against Britain. Some people wanted an immediate break with Britain, but others argued that this step should be taken as a last resort.

In September 1774 the Continental Congress met in Philadelphia to debate this and other options.

*Right* Benjamin Franklin drew this cartoon to show the dangers of colonial disunity in the French and Indian War. He argued for the same unity against Britain.

S.C.   V.   M.   P.   N.E.   N.Y.   N.J.   N.C.

D     E     F     G     H

Fort Albany

Fort Rupert

Moose Factory

*Albany*

*Harricana*

Nova Scotia

Halifax

**Rupert's Land**
(Hudson's Bay Company)

Quebec
created 1763

Québec

William Howe, 1776

Lord Howe, 1776

**CANADA**

Montréal

Burgoyne, 1777

Montgomery, 1775

Arnold, 1775

Falmouth

Fort Népigon

1775

St Leger, 1777

Fort Ticonderoga

Bunker Hill 1775

William Howe, 1776

Fort William

*Lake Superior*

Sault St Marie

Saratoga 1777

Lexington 1775

Boston

Bennington 1777

Providence

**Canada**
1774 to Quebec

*Lake Huron*

*Lake Michigan*

*Lake Ontario*

Fort Stanwix

Fort Oswego

Oriskany 1777

Rochambeau, 1780

White Plains 1776

Rochambeau, 1780

Fort Niagara

Butler, 1778

*Lake Erie*

New York

Long Island 1776

Washington, 1777

Trenton 1776

Monmouth 1778

Princeton 1777

Fort Pontchartrain

Valley Forge

Germantown 1777

de Barras, 1781

Brandywine 1777

**ATLANTIC
OCEAN**

Hamilton, 1778

Fort Sandusky

Fort Pitt

Philadelphia

Baltimore

Washington, 1781

Lafayette, 1781

William Howe, 1777

Yorktown 1781

Fort Vincennes

Clark, 1778–79

*Ohio*

Boonesborough

Richmond

Petersburg

Chesapeake Capes 1781

St Louis

Cahokia

Harrodsburg

**Thirteen
Colonies**

Cornwallis, 1781

de Grasse, 1781

Kakaskia

**Native American Territory**

**A P P A L A C H I A N   M T S**

Guilford Court House 1781

Cornwallis, 1781

Greene, 1781

**Louisiana**
1763 to Spain from France

*Tennessee*

King's Mountain 1780

Cowpens 1781

Hobkirk's Hill 1781

Camden 1780

Wilmington

Augusta

Lincoln 1779

Eutaw Springs 1781

Clinton & Cornwallis, 1780

Campbell, 1778

Charleston

Arkansas Post

*Mississippi*

*Alabama*

*Chattahoochee*

Savannah

Prevost, 1778–79

Fort Rosalie

**West Florida**
created 1764

Pensacola

**East
Florida**

St Augustine

Baton Rouge

New Orleans

British possessions in North America, 1763
- the Thirteen Colonies
- Rupert's Land
- Quebec
- Nova Scotia
- Native American Territory
- Florida
- other

- - - British Proclamation Line of 1763

⌂ fort or trading post

⊗ American victory

⊗ British victory

⊗ French victory

→ American campaign, with commander

→ British campaign, with commander

→ French campaign, with commander

— border of United States of America, 1783

0     600 km
0     400 mi

*Above* "We the People"—the U.S. constitution opens by triumphantly proclaiming the principle of popular will. The ideals of the American Revolution directly inspired other libertarian movements, particularly in France.

*Above* The Declaration of Independence is signed in Philadelphia, July 4, 1776. Its principal author was Thomas Jefferson, a wealthy planter and slave owner who attended the Congress as the representative for Virginia. He later became president (1801–09) and presided over the Louisiana Purchase.

## WAR WITH THE BRITISH

Before the issue had been decided fighting had broken out. Skirmishes between rebel forces and British troops at Lexington and Concord in April 1775 led to a general uprising. On July 4, 1776, the 55 delegates at the Second Continental Congress met to sign the Declaration of Independence.

The British believed that the majority of Americans would remain loyal and that the rebellion would soon be at an end. However, the British generals lacked an effective strategy and failed to make the most of their advantages. The forces the colonists could raise were smaller and vastly more inexperienced, and their morale was often lowered by lack of pay. But the longer the fighting lasted, the more hostile most Americans became to British rule.

In December 1776, Washington led his troops across the frozen Delaware river in a daring raid on the garrison at Trenton. Success began to slip away from the British, who were struggling to supply an army from 3,000 miles away. In 1778 France joined the war against Britain. Their defeat of a British fleet off Chesapeake Capes in 1781 cut off supplies to the British in Yorktown. Its surrender brought the war to an end. At the Treaty of Paris in 1783, Britain recognized the United States of America.

## THE U.S. CONSTITUTION

Once the war was ended, debate started on the way the government of the United States should be organized. In 1786–87 the Constitutional Convention met at Philadelphia to debate these issues. Collectively

Missouri

Colorado

**Vice-Royalty of
New Spain**
to Spain

Rio Grande

known as the Framers of the Constitution, the delegates included Benjamin Franklin and George Washington. At the heart of the debate was the question of how much power should be given to the national government, and how much freedom the individual states should have to govern themselves. It was probably the first time in history that the nature and function of government had been so fully discussed.

A system of "checks and balances" was devised that prevented any single part of the government from growing too powerful. There would be an elected executive head of state (the president), who would not have power to make laws—this would be the prerogative of the two Houses of Congress (the legislature), whose representatives would also be elected. The Supreme Court (the judiciary), independent of both the executive and the legislature, would interpret American law.

The American constitution was one of the first written constitutions of the 18th century. Four years after it was ratified, the first ten amendments, collectively known as the Bill of Rights, were made to the constitution. Some legal scholars consider this to be the most important document in American history as it defines the rights of individual citizens and puts specific limits on government power over the citizen. Today, these issues are once again the subject of debate and controversy as the pressure of social change makes the problems of government more complicated.

## THE UNION GROWS

The new constitution was ratified in 1788, and took effect in 1789, with George Washington as the first president. All 13 colonies had joined the republic by 1790; Rhode Island was the last to do so. Expansion was soon taking place westward along the Ohio river, and Kentucky was incorporated into the Union in 1792, followed by Tennessee and two other states. In 1800 the Mississippi basin was ceded back to France by Spain. In 1803, Napoleon, short of cash to fight his European wars (see pages 36–39), sold the entire territory to the United States. The Louisiana Purchase all but doubled the size of the fledgling republic.

U.S. EXPANSION TO 1803

Rupert's Land to Hudson's Bay Company

Upper Canada to Britain

Lower Canada to Britain

Lake Superior

Lake Huron

Lake Michigan

Lake Ontario

Lake Erie

Vermont 1791

to Massachusetts

New Hampshire 1788

Massachusetts 1788

Rhode Island 1790

New York 1785–90

Connecticut 1788

New York 1788

Pennsylvania 1787

Philadelphia 1790–1800

New Jersey 1787

Northwest Territory

Ohio 1803

Washington from 1800

Delaware 1787

Louisiana

Mississippi

Missouri

Platte

Ohio

Virginia 1788

Maryland 1788

Kentucky 1792

ATLANTIC OCEAN

Arkansas

Tennessee 1796

North Carolina 1789

Red

Mississippi Territory

South Carolina 1788

Georgia 1788

Florida to Spain

Gulf of Mexico

expansion of the United States

- Thirteen Colonies
- 1783 settlement and Native American cessions
- Louisiana Purchase, 1803

**1787** date of admission of state to the Union

■ United States capital

— borders, 1803

# THE EUROPEAN REFORMATION

BY THE 16TH CENTURY THE CATHOLIC CHURCH, WHICH HAD DOMINATED WESTERN EUROPE FOR A THOUSAND YEARS, HAD BECOME CORRUPT. INDIVIDUAL VOICES CALLED FOR REFORM, WHILE POWERFUL MONARCHS CHALLENGED ROME'S POLITICAL AUTHORITY. THE RELIGIOUS AND CIVIL CONFLICTS OF THE TIME SET NEIGHBOR AGAINST NEIGHBOR.

Kings in 16th-century Europe were more powerful than their predecessors. The 15th century had been a time of dynastic civil wars, but the rise of an educated class of professional bureaucrats had increased the efficiency of royal governments, while international bankers made it possible for kings to pay for fulltime armies with which to coerce their subjects. European culture was changing as Renaissance humanist thinkers challenged the certainties of medieval theology and questioned the role of rulers.

*Right* A satirical cartoon showing the head of Martin Luther being used as a bagpipe to play the Devil's tune.

## ROYAL RIVALS

In an age of fierce competition between monarchs, the most powerful ruler in Europe was Charles V (Charles I of Spain). He was only 19 years old when he was elected Holy Roman emperor on the death of his grandfather Maximilian I in 1519, and so added to his Spanish possessions those of the Habsburg empire—Austria, Bohemia, Hungary, Burgundy, the Netherlands, and much of Italy. His wealth was made still greater by the steady stream of silver and gold that entered his coffers from the Spanish empire in Mexico and Peru.

Not unnaturally, other European rulers resented his superiority. His greatest rival was the French king Francis I (r.1515–57), whose lands were almost entirely surrounded by Habsburg territories. Francis had unsuccessfully opposed Charles in elections for Holy Roman emperor, and his attempts to extend French influence into northern Italy were fiercely resisted by Charles; their wars threatened to destroy the achievements of the Italian Renaissance. For a year, after the battle of Pavia (1525), Francis was Charles' prisoner. Francis had a highly competitive relationship with Henry VIII of England (r.1509–47). The two came face to face at a meeting called the Field of the Cloth of Gold (1520), when Francis' entourage far outshone Henry's in wealth and splendor. A great Renaissance prince, Francis employed Italian artists and architects, including Leonardo da Vinci, to build and embellish his palaces.

*Above* The ideas of the Reformation spread quickly through the new printing presses.

## RELIGIOUS CONFLICT

Charles V's greatest problems lay within his own empire. He was a devout Catholic, but the church, especially in Germany, had become deeply unpopular with many of his subjects. Priests used their positions for

1517–1598
borders, 1600
predominantly Catholic, 1598
Protestant lands reverting to Catholicism by 1600
Protestant/Reformed
predominantly Calvinist/Huguenot, 1598
predominantly Church of England, 1598
predominantly Lutheran, 1598
lands with mixed Calvinist/Catholic/Lutheran faiths, 1598
Ottoman empire, 1492
Ottoman gains by 1600
major center of St Bartholomew massacre, 1572
major printing center, 15th–16th centuries
Ottoman offensive against Christian Europe
campaign of Don John, 1571
0
600 km
0
400 mi
North Sea
SWEDEN
Vänern
Vättern
Gotland
DENMARK–NORWAY
ESTONIA
Lake Peipus
Livonia
LATVIA
Courland
Baltic Sea
LITHUANIA
PRUSSIA
POLAND
Vistula
Warsaw
Emden
Hamburg
Netherlands
Amsterdam
Deventer
Utrecht
London
HOLY ROMAN EMPIRE
Elbe
Brandenburg
Berlin
GERMANY
Anhalt
Wittenberg
Leipzig
Saxony
Lusatia
Silesia
Antwerp
Brussels
Cologne
Bonn
Hesse-Kassel
BELGIUM
Nassau
Mainz
Frankfurt
Bamberg
Prague
Luxembourg
Nuremberg
Upper Palatinate
Bohemia
Lower Palatinate
Ansbach
Moravia
Rouen
Meaux
Paris
Strasbourg
IMPERIAL HUNGARY
Troyes
Bavaria
Augsburg
Munich
Danube
Vienna
1529
Orléans
Basel
Austria
Guns
Buda
Bourges
Franche Comté
Zürich
Berne
Swiss Confederation
Tyrol
HUNGARY
1532
1526
Charolais
FRANCE
Geneva
SLOVENIA
TRANSYLVANIA
Lyon
Savoy
Milan
Venice
CROATIA
ROMANIA
Rhône
Po
Parma
VENICE
Belgrade
WALLACHIA
Genoa
Modena
Ravenna
BOSNIA HERZEGOVINA
Avignon
Genoa
PAPAL STATES
URBINO
Black Sea
Aix
Florence
YUGOSLAVIA
Toulouse
Tuscany
Montenegro
Bulgaria
Siena
ANDORRA
Corsica to Genoa
Subiaco
Rome
ITALY
OTTOMAN EMPIRE
Constantinople
Barcelona
NAPLES
Naples
Thessalonica
Rumelia
BENEVENTO
SARDINIA
Sardinia
GREECE
ANATOLIA
TURKEY
Balearic Islands
1537
1543–44
Reggio
Lepanto 1571
SICILY
Morea
1522
Sicily
Algiers
Mediterranean Sea
1543
Malta
1530
Rhodes
Crete to Venice

personal gain, and the popes themselves were seen to be more concerned with politics than with spiritual leadership. One of the most detested abuses was the sale of "indulgences," which allowed the rich to buy forgiveness of their sins. In 1517 a former monk and theologian, Martin Luther (1483–1546), composed a lengthy protest against these practices, which he nailed to the door of the university church in Wittenberg for everyone to read; they are known as the 95 Theses. It was a courageous act: those disagreeing with the church could be condemned as heretics and burned alive.

Printed copies of the 95 Theses spread quickly, and soon Germany and all Europe was immersed in the religious debate of the Reformation. Luther was outlawed by an imperial court at Worms in 1521, but support for his views continued to grow. Other reformers inside and outside Germany took his ideas in new directions. The most influential of them was the Frenchman John Calvin (1509–64), founder of Calvinism.

By the 1530s a great number of German princes were Protestants (the name given to members of the reformed churches). This was often more for reasons of politics than religion: it enabled them to declare their independence from the emperor, and made them rich from the seizure of church lands. Charles failed to bring the princes back to the Catholic faith, and at the Peace of Augsburg (1555) conceded their right to decide what faith their subjects should follow. Believing he had failed in his religious duty, he divided his empire in two and retired to a monastery. His son Philip II was given Spain, the Netherlands, Naples, Sicily and Sardinia, his brother Ferdinand II Austria, Hungary, and Bohemia.

## REFORM SPREADS

The weakening of papal authority was evident in the willingness of many European rulers to break with Rome for reasons of state. One of the first to do so was king Gustavus Vasa of Sweden, who took all church property in his kingdom into his own hands in 1527. In 1534 Henry VIII made himself supreme head of the church in England after the pope had refused to grant him a divorce so that he could marry Anne Boleyn, the second of his six wives.

The Catholic Church had been comparatively slow to meet the challenge of the new reformed ideas, but in 1545 a general council met at Trent in southern Austria to launch the Counter Reformation. Catholic teaching was redefined, Protestant literature banned, and in Catholic countries the medieval Inquisition was revived to track down and interrogate Protestants. The missionary Jesuit order, founded in Spain in 1540, had particular success in bringing people back to the Catholic faith, especially in Bavaria, Austria, and Poland.

Despite this, Protestantism continued to spread. In the 1560s Calvinism, more radical and uncompromising in its beliefs than Lutheranism, gained hold in the Netherlands, Switzerland, Scotland, and much of France (where its followers were known as Huguenots). In England, Puritanism was also influenced by Calvinism. The Counter Reformation needed a new champion.

## WARS OF RELIGION

It found its champion in Philip II of Spain (r.1556–98). A dour, earnest ruler, he was more than ready to take up his father's war against Protestantism. His harsh measures led to rebellion in the Netherlands. By 1566 this had became an outright struggle for Dutch independence, effectively gained in 1609. The Dutch were aided by Elizabeth of

# THE MONSTROUS REGIMENT OF WOMEN

*M*en in the 16th century were often unwilling to accept women as rulers, believing that God had endowed them with natural authority over women. One of those most opposed to women rulers was the Scottish Calvinist preacher, John Knox (1514–72). In the 1550s three women occupied European thrones—Mary I of Scotland (Mary Queen of Scots), Mary Tudor in England, and Catherine de Medici in France. All three were Catholic monarchs, set on persecuting

*Left  Elizabeth I of England, painted in 1588.*

Protestants in their realms. Knox furiously condemned them in a pamphlet entitled "The First Blast of the Trumpet against the Monstrous Regiment of Women," but unfortunately for him, its publication coincided with the death of Mary Tudor and the accession of her formidable Protestant sister, Elizabeth. She once famously said "I know I have the body of a weak and feeble woman, but I have the heart and stomach of a king." Incensed by Knox's misogyny, Elizabeth had him banned from England for life.

## THE HABSBURG EMPIRE

- Austrian Habsburg lands, 1600
- Spanish Habsburg lands, 1600
- Spanish military route
- Spanish Armada, 1588
- return journey, 1600
- under Dutch control

SCOTLAND

ENGLAND

1588
Dunkirk

Netherlands
HOLY
ROMAN
EMPIRE

Luxembourg
Franche-
Comté

Bohemia

*Danube*

Tyrol   Austria

HUNGARY

FRANCE

Milan
Finale

OTTOMAN
EMPIRE

La Coruña

SPAIN
Madrid

NAPLES

Lisbon

SARDINIA

Naples

*Mediterranean
Sea*

Cádiz

SICILY

England (r. 1558–1603), who had restored Protestantism after Mary Tudor's brief and bloody reimposition of Catholicism (1553–58). In retaliation, Philip sent a huge fleet, the Spanish Armada, to invade England in 1588. It was a complete failure, destroyed more by bad weather than the English navy.

In France, a long civil war broke out after the Huguenots took up arms in 1562. The Catholics, who had the support of the king, Philip II, committed one of the very worst atrocities of the European wars of religion

*Left  Protestant nobles, in Paris for the wedding of Henry of Navarre, are massacred by Catholics.*

by killing thousands of Huguenots in the St. Bartholomew's Day Massacre (1572). In 1598 Henry IV, a Protestant who became Catholic in order to pacify the kingdom, granted Huguenots freedom of conscience through the Edict of Nantes.

The same year Philip died. Spain by now was bankrupt, its supplies of silver exhausted by Philip's wars. Some 40% of Europe's population was Protestant. Despite a spectacular naval victory at Lepanto by Philip's half-brother Don John in 1571, the Turks were still a threat to Europe (see page 44). Tunis was lost three years later, and their attacks continued in eastern Europe.

## TIMETABLE

**1517**
Martin Luther nails his 95 Theses to the door of Wittenberg cathedral

**1519**
Charles of Habsburg, king of Spain since 1516, is elected Holy Roman emperor

**1521**
Charles V outlaws Luther at a formal church council in Germany called the Diet of Worms

**1529**
The Ottoman Turks lay unsuccessful siege to Vienna

**1534**
Henry VIII makes himself head of the Church in England

**1536**
John Calvin publishes *The Institutes of the Christian Religion*

**1545–63**
The Council of Trent launches the Counter Reformation

**1555**
The Peace of Augsburg allows German princes to decide the religion of their subjects

**1559**
The Treaty of Cateau-Cambresis ends Italian wars between France and Spain

**1572**
On St. Bartholomew's Day, French Catholics massacre Huguenots

**1576**
Spanish troops slaughter 7,000 people at the siege of Antwerp

**1580**
Philip II becomes king of Portugal

**1587**
Mary Queen of Scots is executed on the order of Elizabeth I of England

**1588**
Philip II sends the Spanish Armada against England

**1598**
The Edict of Nantes grants Huguenots toleration in France

**1609**
A 12-year truce is agreed between the Netherlands and Spain

# EUROPE IN CONFLICT

RELIGIOUS CONFLICT CONTINUED TO AGITATE EUROPE IN THE 17TH CENTURY AND WAS THE CAUSE OF THE CATACLYSMIC THIRTY YEARS WAR (1618–48). BY THE CENTURY'S END, RELIGION WAS LOSING ITS DIVISIVE NATURE. THE FRANCE OF LOUIS XIV WAS NOW THE MAJOR POLITICAL FORCE IN EUROPE, DOMINATING ITS NEIGHBORS BY WAR AND INTIMIDATION.

The split between Roman Catholics and Protestants dominated all other issues in Europe at the start of the 17th century— both sides were resolutely hostile and conspiracies were seen everywhere. The Peace of Augsburg (1555), intended to establish the means of coexistence between Catholic and Protestant rulers in the Holy Roman empire, had failed because neither side trusted the other. The immediate cause of the Thirty Years War was the attempt by the Habsburg rulers of Austria to reimpose Roman Catholicism in their territories in Bohemia in 1618. The war dragged on until 1648 and drew in most of Europe.

In the first stage of fighting (1618–23) the Spanish Habsburgs invaded the Lower Palatinate, the leading Protestant state in Germany, in support of Austria. Then Denmark intervened on the side of the German Protestants until defeated at Lutter (1625–29). Gustavus II Adolphus of Sweden fared

better for a time and briefly carried the war to the heart of Catholic Germany (1630–35). In the war's final phase (1635–48) France, a Catholic country surrounded by Habsburg lands, supported the Swedish–Protestant side. In France's foreign affairs, political differences had more weight than religion, but Huguenots were still disadvantaged at home, despite the Edict of Nantes.

The Thirty Years War had lasting disastrous consequences for Germany. Most soldiers in the war were mercenaries, often left unpaid for long periods. They destroyed vast areas of the countryside, leaving the population to starve—it fell by 7 million.

Spain's days as Europe's leading power were finished. France won some major battles, but domestic rebellions prevented it from exploiting its gains. The only beneficiary of the war was the Netherlands. Spain finally recognized its independence in the Treaty of Westphalia, which ended the war. Dutch ships had taken over Spanish and Portuguese trade routes, and Amsterdam was now the financial center of Europe.

*Below* A military skirmish during the Thirty Years War—the conflict caused tremendous devastation.

## Habsburgs and allies
- Austrian Habsburg territory, 1618
- Spanish Habsburg territory, 1618
- other states, 1618

## states hostile to Habsburgs
- France, 1618
- German Protestant states
- United Provinces, 1609
- Sweden, 1618
- allied states
- other Catholic lands
- other Protestant lands
- borders, 1648

## theater of war
- Bohemian War, 1618–23
- Danish War, 1625–29
- Swedish War, 1630–35
- Franco–Swedish War, 1635–48
- Gustavus Adolphus, 1631–32
- ⊗ Habsburg and imperialist victory
- ⊗ Protestant alliance/French victory

## English civil war
- ⊗ royalist victory
- ⊗ parliamentary victory
- controlled by parliamentarians, Dec 1645
- campaign of Oliver Cromwell
- area granted to veterans of Cromwell's army, 1651

0      400 km
0      300 mi

1600–1715

Stockholm

*Vänern*
*Vättern*

SWEDEN

North
Sea

Baltic Sea

DENMARK–NORWAY

Scotland
Aberdeen
Edinburgh
Philiphaugh 1645

Ulster
Belfast

Drogheda
Dublin

Marston Moor 1644 York
Hull

1650–51

England
Nottingham
Naseby 1645
Edgehill 1642
Gloucester Oxford
Bristol
Roundway Down 1643
Newbury 1643
Turnham Green 1643
London
Lostwithiel 1644

Wexford

Copenhagen

Königsberg PRUSSIA
Danzig

West Pomerania Stralsund
Holstein

Bremen
Mecklenburg

East Pomerania

Brandenburg

Vistula

Elbe

Frankfurt

POLAND

Dunkirk
Spanish Netherlands
Brussels

UNITED PROVINCES
Amsterdam

Kleve
Mark

Ravensberg
Westphalia

Anhalt

Saxony

Lutter 1626
Lützen 1632
Breitenfeld 1631

Silesia

Krakow

Rouen

Rocroi 1643

HOLY ROMAN EMPIRE
Frankfurt

Hesse

Bayreuth

White Mountain 1620
Bohemia Prague

CZECH REPUBLIC

Oder

Paris

Lower Palatinate
Rhine
Württemberg

Ansbach

Moravia

Orléans

Loire

Bourges

Nantes

Breisach
Munich
Bavaria

Danube

Austria
Vienna

AUSTRIA

Gran
Buda

IMPERIAL HUNGARY

TRANSYLVANIA

Charolais

FRANCE

Franche Comté

SWISS CONFEDERATION

Tyrol
Salzburg

Styria

Carinthia

HUNGARY

Bay of Biscay

Bordeaux

Lyon
Rhône

Geneva

SAVOY

Turin
Po

MILAN
Milan
Mantua

Carniola

CROATIA

Venice
VENICE

OTTOMAN EMPIRE

Bilbao
Pamplona

Toulouse

Avignon

Marseille

Genoa
GENOA

PARMA
MODENA

Ravenna

PAPAL STATES

Montenegro

Santander

Perpignan
Roussillon 1642 to France

ANDORRA

Florence
TUSCANY

Ragusa

ITALY

Barcelona

PIOMBINO

Corsica to Genoa

Rome

BENEVENTO
Naples

NAPLES

ALBANIA

Valencia

Palma

Balearic Islands

Sardinia
SARDINIA
Cagliari

Mediterranean Sea

Palermo
Messina

SICILY

Sicily

MALTA

*Left* Oliver Cromwell failed to find an alternative to royal power and finished up almost a king himself.

## ENGLAND'S CIVIL WAR

Although England stayed out of the Thirty Years War, it did not avoid religious and political dispute. Like other European monarchs, Charles I (r.1625–49) believed that kings ruled by divine right. His attempts to govern without Parliament alienated many of his subjects; his religious policies offended English Puritans and Scots Calvinists. The result was civil war. Charles lost, and was executed in 1649. A Commonwealth was set up under Oliver Cromwell, who later took the title of Lord Protector (1653) and ruled as a military dictator. The monarchy was restored in 1660, two years after his death, but on terms that Parliament dictated to the new king, Charles II.

The Glorious Revolution of 1688–89 set the Dutch king William of Orange (married to James II's daughter Mary) on the English throne and barred Catholics from succeeding. At the same time, the Bill of Rights put further restrictions on royal power. In 1707 the Act of Union formally joined the kingdoms of England and Scotland to form the United Kingdom of Great Britain.

## IN THE COURT OF THE SUN KING

Louis XIV's title of the "Sun King" owed much to the splendor of the vast palace he built for himself at Versailles, near Paris. The cost of this project, one of the masterpieces of European architecture, accounted for 5% of France's gross annual income—it has been compared to the expense of constructing a modern airport. The palace was embellished by the finest architects and artists of the day. More than 1,400 fountains played in the palace's grounds. Spectacular ballets, lavish concerts, and firework displays added to Versailles' glories.

From 1682 Louis lived most of the time at Versailles, and expected his nobles to do so too. The king was continually on display at Versailles, which became the center of the French universe. The great nobles of France scrambled with each other for the privilege of attending the semipublic ritual of his rising in the morning and going to bed at night. To be asked to hold the king's shirt was considered a great honor. This fierce competition for the king's favor enabled Louis to play off rivalries between courtiers and keep even his most powerful subjects firmly in check. Despite Versailles' surface brilliance, however, basic amenities for courtiers were few, and living quarters were notoriously cramped.

*Right* The landscaped gardens at Versailles were one of the glories of the age.

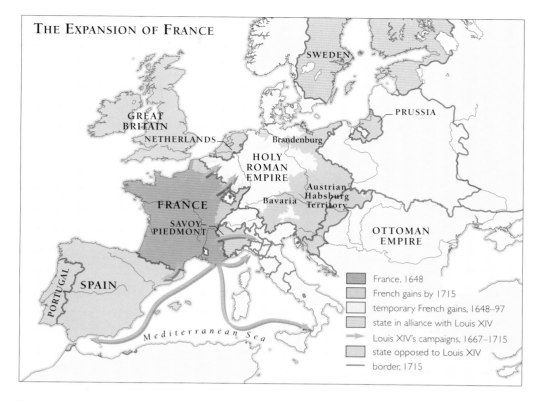

## THE EXPANSION OF FRANCE

SWEDEN

PRUSSIA

GREAT
BRITAIN

NETHERLANDS

Brandenburg

HOLY
ROMAN
EMPIRE

Austrian
Habsburg
Territory

FRANCE

Bavaria

SAVOY-
PIEDMONT

OTTOMAN
EMPIRE

PORTUGAL

SPAIN

*Mediterranean Sea*

France, 1648
French gains by 1715
temporary French gains, 1648–97
state in alliance with Louis XIV
Louis XIV's campaigns, 1667–1715
state opposed to Louis XIV
border, 1715

# THE RISE OF FRANCE

In contrast to England, the power of the French monarchy grew much stronger during the reign of Louis XIV (1643–1715, the longest in European history). He succeeded to the throne at the age of four, and his early years were made wretched by civil war and intrigue among the French aristocracy. He determined that the crown should exercise absolute authority to prevent this ever happening again.

Louis had ambitions to make France the greatest power in Europe. In 1661 he took the rule of the kingdom into his own hands and, with the help of skilled advisers, set about reforming the government, the army, and the navy. He then successfully attacked Spain and the Netherlands, winning valuable new territories for France.

Other European states were made nervous by Louis' aggression. Any chance he had of forming military alliances with Protestant countries was spoiled when he outlawed the Huguenots in 1685 by revoking the Edict of Nantes. This caused general alarm as no one wanted to see the old religious wars start up once more. Some 200,000 Huguenots fled abroad, to the detriment of the French economy. Most were skilled craftsmen and merchants; a large number of them took their skills and expertise to England and the Dutch Republic.

Louis' subjects were heavily taxed to pay for his wars. Resentment of the king began to grow but, isolated at Versailles and convinced of his divine right to rule, he ignored it. His successors carried on in the same way, adding to the grievances that led to the French Revolution (see pages 32–35).

# THE SPANISH SUCCESSION

Louis' last and most ambitious scheme was in Spain. He managed to persuade the childless Spanish king Charles II to accept Louis' teenage grandson Philip as his heir. When he became king on Charles' death in 1700, Louis refused to exclude him from the succession to the French throne. The fear that France would eventually control Spain, its American empire, the Spanish Netherlands, and much of Italy led almost all Europe, including Britain, to back the Austrian Habsburg candidate in the War of the Spanish Succession (1701–13). Louis suffered a number of military defeats and sought to end the war. The Treaty of Utrecht ended Spain's role as a European power. Philip was confirmed as Spanish king, but had to give up all territories outside Spain to Austria. Louis was forced to promise that the French and Spanish crowns would never be united. Britain took possession of Spanish and French trading bases in the Caribbean, boosting its overseas empire.

## TIMETABLE

**1610**
Henry IV of France is assassinated by a fanatic

**1618**
The Thirty Years War begins

**1624**
Cardinal Richelieu becomes chief minister of France

**1632**
Gustavus II Adolphus of Sweden is killed at the battle of Lutzen

**1648**
The Treaty of Westphalia ends the Thirty Years War

**1649**
Charles I of England is executed by Parliament and a Commonwealth established

**1660**
Charles II is restored as king of England

**1661**
Louis XIV begins to rule France directly

**1666**
Much of the city of London is destroyed in a great fire

**1669**
Portugal regains its independence from Spain

**1672**
William of Orange floods much of the Dutch Netherlands to save them from French invasion

**1683**
A Polish army led by John Sobieski breaks the Turkish siege of Vienna

**1685**
Louis XIV revokes the Edict of Nantes, ending toleration of Huguenots

**1699**
Austria annexes Hungary from the Turks

**1707**
The Act of Union unites Scotland and England as Great Britain

**1713**
The Treaty of Utrecht ends the War of Spanish Succession

**1715**
Louis XIV dies and is succeeded by his 5-year-old great-grandson, Louis XV

# THE AGE OF ENLIGHTENMENT

POLITICAL AND ECONOMIC DEVELOPMENTS IN 18TH-CENTURY EUROPE
CHANGED THE COURSE OF WORLD HISTORY. THE FRENCH REVOLUTION
THREW THE WHOLE CONTINENT INTO POLITICAL CHAOS AND WARFARE FOR
OVER 20 YEARS, WHILE THE BEGINNING OF THE INDUSTRIAL REVOLUTION IN
BRITAIN BROUGHT NOT ONLY MACHINES AND FACTORIES BUT ALSO SOCIAL
CHANGES AS PROFOUND AS THOSE
OF THE FRENCH REVOLUTION.

The 18th century is often called the Age of the Enlightenment—the name given to a cultural movement that developed partly in reaction to the religious conflicts of the previous century. The study of science (or natural philosophy as it was called) provided experimental proof of a world governed by physical rather than divine laws and seemed to offer a more rational basis for understanding the world than religious belief. The Royal Society of London (1660) was the first body in Europe to be founded for the study of science. A similar society was soon set up in Paris.

Dynastic wars divided the continent in the 1730s and 40s. Austria began to win territory back from the Ottomans, as did Russia later in the century. The Seven Years War (1756–63) saw France, Austria, and Russia joined against Britain and the rising kingdom of Prussia. Although France lost most of its overseas colonies to Britain, it

*Above By the end of the 18th century, the "sans-culottes" ("man without breeches") had become the symbol of the new revolutionary forces in France.*

remained a major power on the continent. It took its revenge by aiding the American colonies in their independence wars against Britain. In eastern Europe, Poland—much reduced in size—ceased to exist as a sovereign state in 1795, having been partitioned between Russia, Prussia, and Austria.

## ABSOLUTIST RULERS

Prussia's rise was engineered by its third king, Frederick the Great (r. 1740–86), a talented military strategist who was admired for his achievements and loathed for his excessive ambition. Frederick was passionately interested in art, music (he played the flute) and philosophy, and was the first European ruler to advocate public education and universal religious tolerance. He was typical of his age, however, in his failure to modify Prussia's rigid social structure. Aristocrats, the new middle classes, and the

## THE INDUSTRIAL REVOLUTION

*The Industrial Revolution began in the 18th century with the invention of mechanized means of spinning yarn. At about the same time, iron manufacture was transformed by the development of the blast furnace. Industrial centers grew up around coalfields and canals were built to move goods in bulk. The coming of steam power speeded up the pace of change still further. Improvements in agriculture meant fewer people were needed to work the land. These events radically altered the way people lived in Britain and parts of northern Europe as more and more people left the countryside to work in the emerging industrial cities.*

*Above A cast iron bridge, built in 1779, spans the river Severn, Britain.*

La Coruña

Oporto

PORTUGAL

Lisbon
1779

Guadiar

Gibraltar
to Britain
Cádiz
Tangier
Ceuta
to Spain

Christiania

**SWEDEN**

Uppsala
1710

Stockholm
1741

Revel

Riga

*Lake
Peipus*

**RUSSIAN
EMPIRE**

*Vänern*

*B
a
l
t
i
c

S
e
a*

*Gotland*

*Vättern*

**DENMARK–NORWAY**

*North
Sea*

Samogitia

*Western Dvina*

Lithuania

Minsk

Falkirk
Edinburgh
1739
Glasgow

**GREAT BRITAIN
& IRELAND**

Hamburg

Hanover

Berlin
1700

**POLAND**

BELARUS

Black
Russia

Bolton   Bury
ublin
1731   Cromford
Iron Bridge   Birmingham
Dudley   1766
London
1660

Haarlem
1752

Rotterdam
1773

NETHERLANDS

Göttingen
1736

GERMANY

**HOLY ROMAN
EMPIRE**

Prague

Warsaw

Great Poland

Little Poland

Podlesia

Volhynia

Red Russia

*Vistula*

Plymouth

Jemappe

Amiens
1750

Mannheim
1755

Munich
1759

Bohemia

Moravia

Galicia and Lodomeria

Silesia

Rouen
1736
Caen
1705   Paris   Plassey
1666   Nancy
1736
Orléans
1753

Reims
1776

*Danube*

*Rhine*

Austria

Vienna

Buda

Hungary

Bukovina

Jassy

Brest

**FRANCE**

Dijon
1723

*Loire*
Nantes

Geneva
1776

**SWISS
CONFEDERATION**

Tyrol

Carinthia

Styria

Transylvania

*Bay of
Biscay*

Clermont-
Ferrand
1705   Lyon
1700

**SARDINIA–
PIEDMONT**

Milan

Padua
1779   Venice

Carniola

Croatia

Slavonia

Banat

ROMANIA

*Sava*

Bordeaux
1712

Venaissin
to Papal States

Genoa

Parma

**VENICE**

*Danube*

Toulouse
1782   Avignon

**GENOA**

Florence
1752

MONTENEGRO

BULGARIA

Marseille
1726

**TUSCANY**   **PAPAL
STATES**

ITALY

RAGUSA

**OTTOMAN
EMPIRE**

**ANDORRA**

*Corsica*

Rome

*Naples*

Constantinople

**PAIN**

*Ebro*

Barcelona

**SARDINIA–
PIEDMONT**

Naples
1779

TURKEY

Madrid
1713

Valencia

*Balearic
Islands*

*Sardinia*

**KINGDOM OF
NAPLES AND
SICILY**

Palermo

GREECE

*Sicily*

Oran

*Crete*

Melilla
to Spain

*Malta*

*M e d i t e r r a n e a n
S e a*

borders, 1789

Austrian Habsburg territory, 1789

France, 1789

Brandenburg–Prussia, 1789

Great Britain & Hanover, 1789

Ottoman empire, 1789

Spanish Bourbon territory, 1789

Russian empire, 1789

Brandenburg–Prussian gains by 1795

Russian gains by 1795

Austrian Habsburg gains by 1797

scientific society, with date of foundation

observatory

important industrial site

0          600 km

0          400 mi

peasantry were firmly fixed in their established places. Most European rulers were absolutists, who supported religious conformism and protected aristocratic privileges. New agricultural techniques (particularly improved methods of crop rotation and livestock breeding) were revolutionizing farming in Britain and the Netherlands but had only limited impact elsewhere; in most of Europe, the labor-intensive institution of serfdom still tied peasants to the land and prevented innovation.

In France the conservative social order, headed by the monarchy and supported by the church, was known as the *ancien régime* (the old regime). The rising middle class, though wealthy and numerous, was excluded from centers of power, which continued to revolve around the court life of Versailles. Increasingly, the narrow, aristocratic values of the *ancien régime* were challenged by the leaders of the Enlightenment, which had its roots among the French middle class. Leading intellectuals such as the great French philosopher-essayist Voltaire attacked the repressive nature of the Catholic church, and tried to persuade rulers to introduce progressive reforms such as the abolition of serfdom and the use of torture.

A passionate belief in the dignity of people—not as the subjects of kings, but as individuals—was one of the touchstones of the Enlightenment, and was strengthened by the success of the American Revolution, which the French had supported. These ideas found their fullest expression in the political and philosophical writings of Jean-Jacques Rousseau (1712–78). His ideas on education profoundly influenced parental attitudes to childcare, and his political treatises, the *Social Contract* (1762) in particular, with its emphasis on individual liberty, helped shape the intellectual background to the debates of the French revolutionaries. Rousseau's attitudes to nature pointed the way ahead to the Romanticism of the early 19th century.

## REVOLUTION IN FRANCE

The cost of France's participation in the American Revolution was a high one. It bankrupted the government, and soaring prices and food shortages caused hardship and panic, giving rise to demands for political reform. The Estates-General, France's representative assembly, had not been summoned since 1614, but in 1789 Louis XVI called it to approve his plans to raise taxes. The Estates-General was made up of three estates, or assemblies: that of the clergy, the nobles, and the commoners. Following an argument about the voting power of each of the estates, the entire Third Estate withdrew and set up a rival National Assembly in Paris to institute reforms.

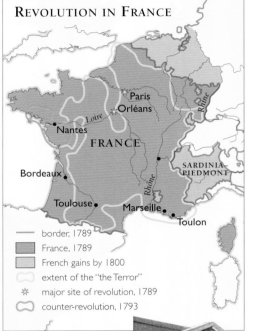

**REVOLUTION IN FRANCE**

- border, 1789
- France, 1789
- French gains by 1800
- extent of the "the Terror"
- ✳ major site of revolution, 1789
- counter-revolution, 1793

*Right* The execution of Marie Antoinette, queen of France, in October 1793. Born into the Habsburg dynasty of Austria, she lived in splendor and isolation from her French subjects, who resented both her nationality and her extravagant lifestyle. Her secret negotiations with Austria against the revolutionaries were the chief factor that led to her execution and that of the indecisive King Louis XVI.

The assembly received widespread popular support. On July 14, 1789, as rumors spread that the king's army was planning to attack it, an angry crowd gathered to storm the fortress of the Bastille, a hated symbol of royal tyranny. It was taken easily and found to hold only a few prisoners, but it proved a rallying point for popular rebellion.

Under the slogan of *Liberté, Egalité, Fraternité* ("Liberty, Equality, Fraternity") the revolution spread rapidly. Widespread famine and unemployment in the countryside helped foment panic, leading to the "Great Fear" (July 20–August 6, 1789) when armed peasants destroyed aristocratic property in a frenzy of hatred. In Paris, the National Assembly proclaimed the Declaration of the Rights of Man, promising freedom of conscience, property, and speech. Serfdom was outlawed, church property confiscated, and hereditary titles abolished.

At first the National Assembly tried to work with the king, but he proved to be an unwilling partner. In 1791 he tried to flee the country with his wife, the even more unpopular Marie Antoinette, but they were stopped and brought back to Paris. Exiled French aristocrats persuaded Prussia and the Austrian empire to invade France. The king and

## VOLTAIRE & THE ENLIGHTENMENT

*Voltaire, real name François-Marie Arouet (1694–1788), was the embodiment of the Enlightenment. One of France's greatest writers, he devoted his life to criticizing tyranny, intolerance, and injustice. His sharp wit got him into trouble; he was imprisoned in the Bastille twice, and spent nearly 30 years in exile from Paris, part of it in England, which he admired for its freedom of thought. In the 1750s, Frederick the Great of Prussia sheltered him in his palace at Sans Souci, and he also corresponded with Catherine the Great of Russia. From 1754 he lived in Switzerland. After the Revolution his remains were reinterred in the Panthéon.*

*Above  Voltaire dictates a letter as he dresses.*

queen were accused of plotting to betray France and were imprisoned. Moderates within the National Assembly tried to spare them the death sentence, but radical sentiment was too strong. Both were guillotined, along with hundreds of aristocrats.

Royalist revolts broke out in the west and parts of southern France. They were quickly suppressed, whereupon the revolutionaries turned on each other in fierce political feuding. As many as 200,000 people may have died during the Terror of 1793 and 1794, most of them in the civil wars, others on the guillotine or in prison. Two prominent victims of the Terror were Georges Danton and Maximilien de Robespierre, leaders of the extreme Jacobin faction, both of whom had been active in setting it up.

## THE REVOLUTION ABROAD

Fear of French agents fomenting popular uprisings abroad hardened European opposition to revolutionary France, and Britain, the Netherlands, and Spain joined Prussia and Austria in a military alliance against the new republic (the Revolutionary Wars, 1792–1802). In spite of its internal chaos, France held out against its enemies, first of all repelling the invasion attempt to restore the monarchy in 1792, and then going on to the offensive itself. A series of victories in 1794–95 culminated in the successful invasion of the Netherlands (ruled by France as the Batavian Republic until 1806). Prussia and Spain made peace, leaving Britain and Austria to carry on the war. Britain maintained its naval supremacy with a series of victories over France, but by 1797 the general Napoleon Bonaparte (see pages 36–39) had emerged as the greatest of the French commanders after brilliant campaigns in Italy and Austria.

# EUROPE UNDER NAPOLEON

A NATIONAL HERO IN FRANCE, NAPOLEON BONAPARTE WAS SEEN BY SOME AS
AN IDEALIST AND REFORMER, BY OTHERS AS A RUTHLESS TYRANT. HIS MILITARY
GENIUS BROUGHT FRENCH POWER TO ITS PEAK BUT HIS HUGE AMBITION
SUCCEEDED IN UNITING EUROPE'S MAJOR POWERS AGAINST HIM. AFTER
15 YEARS OF WAR, NAPOLEON WAS DEFEATED AND SENT INTO EXILE.
AT THE CONGRESS OF VIENNA (1815) THE VICTORIOUS ALLIES
REDREW THE BOUNDARIES OF EUROPE IN
THEIR OWN FAVOR AND STRIPPED FRANCE
OF ITS OVERSEAS COLONIES.

Napoleon was born on the Mediterranean island of Corsica in 1769, the year that
it became part of France. After graduating
from the Paris military academy, he joined
an artillery regiment in the French army.
The French Revolution provided an oppor-
tunity for the brilliant young officer to
rise. He aligned himself with the more
radical revolutionaries and came to
notice at the siege of Toulon (1793)
when, commanding the artillery, he
forced the withdrawal of an Anglo-
Spanish fleet. Three promotions in four
months made him a brigadier general at age
24, but the fall of the radical leader Robespierre led to Napoleon's arrest and brief
imprisonment the next year.

In October 1795 Napoleon suppressed a
royalist rebellion in Paris and was rewarded
with the command of an army in the con-
tinuing war against France's enemies. Leading campaigns in northern Italy and Austria
(1796–97), his military and strategic skills
were displayed to the full as he took on and
defeated Austria's forces. Britain now stood
alone as France's most implacable enemy.
The government urged Napoleon to launch
an invasion across the Channel, but instead
he led an expedition to Egypt, from where
he planned to strike at Britain's most valuable colony, India. He won a decisive battle
over the Mamluke rulers of Egypt, but the
defeat of his fleet at the battle of the Nile
(1798) by the British admiral Nelson cut off
supplies to the French army, forcing it to
surrender. Despite this debacle, Napoleon's
prestige stood higher than ever in France,
where there was great public enthusiasm
for all things Egyptian. Austria, Russia, and
Turkey, encouraged by the defeat, were led
to resume the war against France.

*Left* "Bonaparte
crossing the Alps,"
a painting by Jacques
Louis David,
Napoleon's official
artist, that glorifies his
successful invasion of
Italy in 1796–97.

## CONSUL & EMPEROR

The foundations of the French republic
were extremely shaky. The Directory, the
committee that had governed since 1795,
was weak and unpopular, and in November 1799 Napoleon conspired with
others to overthrow it and replace it with
a three-man consulate. He justified this by
claiming that only a firm hand could hold
France together after the chaos of the revolutionary years. As First Consul, Napoleon
was in effect the military dictator of France.
The nature of his power was only partly
concealed by a new constitution, which was
approved by popular vote in 1800.

Further campaigns in Europe, culminat-
ing in the defeat of Austria at Marengo
(1800), brought the Revolutionary Wars to
an end. With all its allies in Europe defeated, Britain was compelled to sign the Treaty

# 1799–1815

**B** | **C** | **D** | **E** | **F** | **G** | **H** | **I** | **J**

*North Sea*

SWEDEN

DENMARK–NORWAY

Christiania

*Vänern*

*Vättern*

Stockholm

*Baltic Sea*

*Gotland*

FINLAND

ESTONIA

*Lake Peipus*

LATVIA

LITHUANIA

Moscow 1812

Borodino 1812

Maloyaroslavets 1812

*Western Dvina*

Vitebsk 1812

Smolensk 1812

Krasnoi 1812

Kovno

Vilna 1812

Berezina 1812

Minsk

BELARUS

RUSSIAN EMPIRE

Copenhagen 1801, 1807

Swedish Pomerania

Pomerania

Danzig

Eylau 1807

Friedland 1807

East Prussia

PRUSSIA

Amsterdam

Holland

MECKLENBURG-SCHWERIN

Hanover

Munster

WESTPHALIA

Brandenburg

1806–07

Berlin

*Oder*

GRAND DUCHY OF WARSAW

Warsaw

POLAND

Kiev

Kharkov

UKRAINE

London

Lützen 1813

SAXONY

Leipzig 1813

1813

Breslau

Silesia

*Vistula*

Galicia and Lodomeria

*Dnieper*

Waterloo 1815

Brussels

HESSE

BERG

Jena-Auerstädt 1806

Dresden 1813

Bautzen 1813

Prague

WÜRZBURG

Bohemia

Moravia

Austerlitz 1805

SLOVAKIA

*Dniester*

Bessarabia

Paris

1805

WÜRTTEMBERG

Ratisbon 1809

1809

*Danube*

Vienna

Austria

Wagram 1809

Aspern 1809

AUSTRIAN EMPIRE

Bukovina

Orléans

BADEN

Ulm 1805

Munich

Ebersberg 1809

BAVARIA

Salzburg

Styria

Buda

Hungary

Transylvania

ROMANIA

Banat

FRANCE

HELVETIA

SWITZERLAND

*Rhine*

Carinthia

*Illyrian Provinces*

Slavonia

*Sava*

Belgrade

*Below* The Legion d'honneur (Legion of Honor) was created by Napoleon to reward civilian and military achievements. It is still in use today.

Geneva

1797

Lyon

Grenoble

Milan

Marengo 1800

Lodi 1796

ITALY

Venice

BOSNIA HERZEGOVINA

*Danube*

YUGOSLAVIA

MONTENEGRO

BULGARIA

Toulouse 1814

Avignon

1796

Genoa

LUCCA

PIOMBINO

Tuscany

Florence

1808

Marseille

Cannes

*Corsica*

*Elba*

Papal States

Rome

Naples

NAPLES

OTTOMAN EMPIRE

Andorra

Catalonia

Barcelona 1808

*Sardinia*

1798

*Balearic Islands*

Palermo

SICILY

GREECE

Bonaparte, 1798

*Malta* to Britain

*Mediterranean Sea*

Aboukir 1798, 1799

Alexandria

EGYPT

**Legend:**
- borders, 1812
- French empire, 1812
- state dependent on France, 1812
- French ally, 1812
- Ottoman empire, 1812
- Russian empire, 1812
- United Kingdom of Great Britain and Ireland, 1812
- ⊗ French victory
- ⊗ French defeat
- → French campaign
- → Napoleon's escape from Elba, and the Waterloo campaign, 1815

0 ——— 600 km
0 ——— 400 mi

**Left** *Moscow burns in 1812, set on fire by its citizens to deprive Napoleon of booty and supplies.*

**Below** *Delegates to the Congress of Vienna (1814–15) were entertained at night with lavish balls. In this French satire, Russia, Prussia, and Austria dance to the bidding of Castlereagh, the British delegate (in red).*

of Amiens (1802). Napoleon appointed himself consul for life. In 1804 he went a step further and assumed the hereditary title of emperor, securing the succession in the event of his death.

## TYRANT OR REFORMER?

Napoleon had fought for the revolution, but he had a low opinion of the masses. He ignored the slogans "liberty, equality, fraternity" and "the rights of man." However, as First Consul and then emperor, he introduced a program of reforms that still influence France today: local government and the university system were restructured, a national bank founded, and the tax system made more equitable. The reform of French law, begun by the National Convention in 1790, was completed. The Code Napoleon of 1804 built on some of the old revolutionary ideals—a secular state, individual liberty, freedom of conscience—but it also maintained traditional property rights and offered little protection to workers. Women were granted few rights, though they had been active participants in the revolution.

## THE NAPOLEONIC SYSTEM

No sooner had the Revolutionary Wars ended than Napoleon began to increase French influence in the Netherlands, Switzerland, and Italy. He also tried to extend the French empire overseas and attempted to restrict British trade rights. These expansionist policies caused Britain to declare war again in 1803. Austria, Sweden, and Russia followed suit in 1805 but were rapidly defeated. Napoleon proceeded to occupy most of Germany and abolished what was left of the Holy Roman Empire. Prussia joined the war in 1806 but was also beaten. Napoleon now placed his brothers on royal thrones throughout Europe—an action that was much resented and helped to create nationalist resistance. In 1810 Napoleon divorced the childless Josephine in order to marry the 18-year-old archduchess Marie-Louise, daughter of Francis I of Austria, who duly gave birth to a son, the king of Rome (nicknamed L'Aiglon, or the Eaglet).

By 1807 Britain was on its own. British control of the sea left Napoleon unable to attack Britain directly, so he tried to prevent the rest of Europe from trading with it. His efforts proved by and large ineffectual; illicit trade continued and Britain retaliated by blockading European ports. When Portugal refused to comply with the French ban, Napoleon ordered his army to invade. This sparked off revolt in Spain, and a British army commanded by Wellington landed in

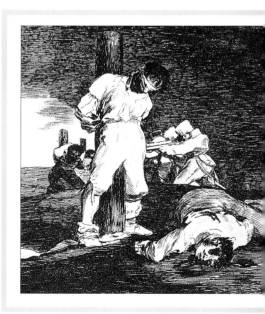

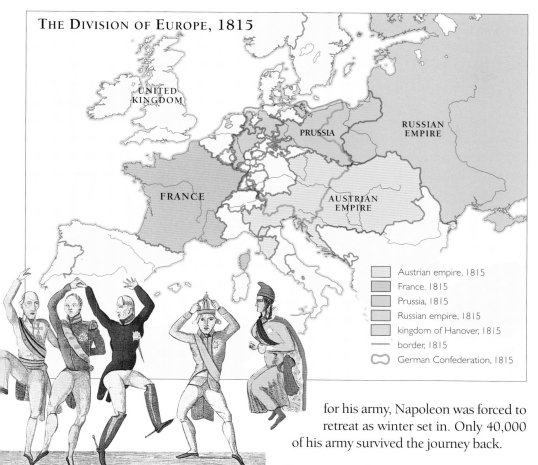

## THE DIVISION OF EUROPE, 1815

UNITED
KINGDOM

PRUSSIA

RUSSIAN
EMPIRE

FRANCE

AUSTRIAN
EMPIRE

- Austrian empire, 1815
- France, 1815
- Prussia, 1815
- Russian empire, 1815
- kingdom of Hanover, 1815
- border, 1815
- German Confederation, 1815

the peninsula to support the rebels. His campaigns succeeded in tying down a large part of the French army. When Russia also ignored the ban Napoleon invaded the country at the head of an army of 600,000 men. He narrowly escaped defeat at Borodino, and went on to capture Moscow, but found it deserted. Unable to find supplies for his army, Napoleon was forced to retreat as winter set in. Only 40,000 of his army survived the journey back.

## DEFEAT & EXILE

Napoleon had been welcomed into many parts of Europe because he was seen as a liberator, spreading the ideals of the French Revolution. But his treatment of the territories he conquered, which were systematically drained of taxes, supplies, and conscripts for the French army, turned the popular mood against him. The catastrophe in Russia persuaded Prussia, Austria, Sweden, and Spain back into the war. As the allies approached Paris, Napoleon abdicated and was exiled to the Italian island of Elba. The French monarchy was restored while the victorious allies met in Vienna to redistribute Napoleon's conquests. Russia eventually emerged with the biggest prize, in the shape of Poland, but Prussia and Austria also made substantial gains.

In March 1815, before the Congress had completed its sessions, Napoleon escaped and returned to France, where he seized power once more. A little more than three months later he was defeated by the British and Prussians at the battle of Waterloo. This time he was exiled to St. Helena in the southern Atlantic, too remote for escape or intrigue, where he died in 1821.

## THE DISASTERS OF WAR

*When Napoleon put his brother Joseph on the Spanish throne in 1808, Madrid rebelled. For the next six years, locally organized militia groups fought the French in a series of skirmishes and raids. The term "guerrilla war" (little war) was invented in this conflict, which was often brutal, with vicious reprisals on both sides. The great Spanish painter Francisco Goya (1746–1828) expressed his feelings of horror in a series of engravings, "The Disasters of War" (1810–14).*

*Left "There is no way out," by Francisco Goya.*

## TIMETABLE

**1793**
Napoleon wins Toulon from the royalists and is made brigadier general

**1796–97**
Napoleon's victories in Italy and Austria win him glory and prestige

**1799**
Napoleon overthrows the Directory and becomes First Consul

**1802**
Napoleon becomes consul for life

**1803**
Britain resumes the war against France. Napoleon threatens to invade Britain

**1804**
Napoleon crowns himself emperor of France in the presence of the pope

**1805**
Nelson's victory at Trafalgar deprives the French of a fleet. Napoleon beats Austria and Russia at Austerlitz

**1806**
Napoleon dissolves the Holy Roman Empire and replaces it with the Confederation of the Rhine

**1807**
The Continental System is introduced

**1808**
Joseph Bonaparte, elder brother of Napoleon, is crowned king of Spain

**1809**
Napoleon enters Vienna and defeats the Austrians at Wagram

**1810**
Napoleon marries Marie-Louise of Austria

**1812**
Napoleon retreats from Russia

**1813**
Napoleon is defeated at Leipzig and leads his army back to France

**1814**
Napoleon abdicates and is exiled to Elba

**1814–15**
The Congress of Vienna meets to reorganize post-Napoleonic Europe

**1815**
After defeat at Waterloo, Napoleon is exiled to St. Helena

# THE EXPANSION OF RUSSIA

FOR 250 YEARS, FROM ABOUT 1240 TO 1480, THE RUSSIAN PRINCIPALITIES WERE SUBJECT TO THE MONGOLIAN TATARS. INDEPENDENCE CAME IN THE REIGN OF IVAN III, GRAND PRINCE OF MOSCOW FROM 1462–1505. HE UNITED THE OTHER PRINCIPALITIES UNDER HIS LEADERSHIP AND BEGAN EXPANDING RUSSIA'S FRONTIERS. BUT RUSSIA REMAINED WEAK AND BACKWARD BY COMPARISON WITH WESTERN EUROPE. MODERN RUSSIA WAS CREATED BY PETER THE GREAT LATE IN THE 17TH CENTURY.

During the centuries of Tatar rule, Moscow looked east, to Persia and central Asia. But the Russians' Orthodox faith linked them to the Byzantine empire. After Byzantium fell to the Ottomans in 1453, Moscow came to be seen as the Third Rome in succession to Constantinople. When Ivan III, grand prince of Moscow, married Zoe, niece of the last Byzantine emperor, he took the double-headed eagle of the Byzantine empire as his own symbol.

The association was made even more explicit by Ivan IV (r.1533–84), who had himself crowned czar (caesar, or emperor) of Russia in 1547. Russia nearly doubled in size during his reign. The Tatars were conquered and Russian control extended into Siberia. However, Ivan's attempts to expand west to the Baltic were resisted by Sweden and Poland. Ivan reduced the power of the nobility (the *boyars*) and took over their estates. During a reign of terror, thousands were killed by his personal bodyguards. This earned him the nickname of "Ivan the Terrible," though "Awe-inspiring" is a more accurate translation of the Russian.

The "Time of Troubles" (1604–13) saw much of western Russia devastated by a civil war, which was ended by the accession of the first Romanov czar (the dynasty that ruled Russia until 1917). Settlement continued to spread eastward down the rivers of Siberia, and Russians had reached the Pacific by 1637. Trading posts were set up and furs became Russia's most valuable export. However, Russia's vast size was not to its advantage; though rich in natural resources, there were enormous problems of communication and transportation, and labor was short. To meet this, serfdom was introduced; peasants lost their traditional right to change employers once a year and were bound for life to one owner or estate

under conditions little different from slavery. Russian nobles were virtually the serfs of the czars. Trade and cultural contact with Europe rose during the 16th century, and there was a flourishing community of westerners—merchants, craftsmen, artists, clergy, and intellectuals—living in Moscow. But, in economic and political terms, Russia still lagged far behind its European neighbors.

*Above* Peter the Great ordered the nobles to shave.

## PETER THE GREAT

The reign of Peter the Great (1682–1725) proved a turning point in Russian history. Although he was not the first czar to introduce westernizing measures (his three predecessors had each done so in a small measure) Peter was the first to attempt to turn Russia into a modern European power, and had the energy and ruthlessness to realize his ambition. In 1697–98 he made a tour

RUSSIA'S PROGRESS EAST

ARCTIC OCEAN

Russian America

Bering Strait

Ob

Tobolsk 1587

Turukhansk 1607

Yenisey

Lena

Nizhnekolymsk 1644

Tomsk 1604

Yeniseysk 1619

Krasnoyarsk 1628

Yakutsk 1632

1648

Olekminsk 1635

Petropavlovsk 1740

Semipalatinsk 1718

Irkutsk 1652

Amur

returned to China following 1689 Treaty of Nerchinsk

MANCHU CHINA

Beijing

Russia, 1689

Russian expansion under Peter the Great, 1689–1725

Russian expansion, 1725–1796

Russian expansion, 1796–1826

border, 1826

new Russian town, with date of foundation

major trade route

DENMARK–NOR...

Zaandam Aug 1697– Jan 1698

Deptford Jan–May 1698

NETHERLANDS

Amsterdam May 1698

Paris

FRANCE

Rhine

SWISS CONFEDERATION

# 1480–1815

**Barents Sea**

SWEDEN

Finland

Karelia

to Europe

Obdorsk 1595

Berezov 1593

Surgut 1594

*Ob*

Archangel 1583

*Eastern Dvina*

Yarensk

Pelym 1592

Solikamskaya

Tobolsk 1587

*Irtysh*

Ingria

*Lake Ladoga*

Olonets

Kargopol

Ustyug

Verkhotyure 1598

Tyumen 1586

Ishim 1670

Omsk 1716

Helsinki

*Lake Onega*

St Petersburg 1703

Vyatka

Yegoshika (Perm)

*Vänern*

Stockholm

Revel

Narva

Estonia

Vologda

*Vättern*

*Lake Peipus*

Pskov

Novgorod

*Volga*

Yaroslavl

Nizhniy Novgorod

Kazan

Ufa 1586

hristiania

Livonia

Riga

Pskov

Tver

Simbirsk 1648

Orenburg 1743

*Oral*

openhagen

Libau

*Western Dvina*

Vitebsk

Moscow

Tula

Tambov 1636

*Baltic Sea*

Königsberg June–July 1697

Smolensk

to Europe

RUSSIA

Saratov 1590

Turgay

Danzig

Minsk

Mogilev

Orel 1564

*Don*

KAZAKHSTAN

*Vistula*

POLAND

Voronezh 1586

Warsaw

USSIA

*Oder*

Ukraine

Kiev

Kharkov 1654

Tsaritsyn 1589

Guryev 1645

Krakow

UKRAINE

Podolia

*Dnieper*

*Volga*

Astrakhan

*Aral Sea*

Lemberg (Lvov)

Vienna June–July 1698

Jassy

Azov

KHANATE OF CRIMEA

Kinburn

Kaffa

Kerch

UZBEKISTAN

*Amu Darya*

AUSTRIAN EMPIRE

HUNGARY

Sevastopol 1783

*Sava*

*Danube*

ROMANIA

Varna

*Black Sea*

CAUCASUS MTS

Derbent

*Caspian Sea*

Khiva

BULGARIA

Georgia

Batum

Tiflis

Baku

TURKMENISTAN

Constantinople

Yerevan

PLES

GREE

OTTOMAN EMPIRE

TURKEY

Tabriz

Gorgan

Meshed

IRAQ

Tehran

PERSIA

IRAN

Russia, 1505

Russia by 1689

Russian expansion under Peter the Great, 1689–1725

Russian expansion by the death of Catherine II, 1796

Russian expansion, 1796–1815

Polish territory at maximum extent, 1618–34

borders, 1815

new Russian town, with date of foundation

route of Peter the Great, 1697–98

major trade route

0        600 km
0        400 mi

of Prussia, the Netherlands, England, and Austria to teach himself about the technology of the west, particularly shipbuilding (he even worked as a shipwright in England and Holland). On returning home, he set about reorganizing the Russian army and in 1700 went to war with Sweden to win an outlet on the Baltic, where he founded his new capital of St. Petersburg. English and Dutch shipwrights were imported to supervise the building of a modern navy, while Italian architects introduced the fashionable baroque style to Russia. State-run copper and ironworks were founded in the Urals to exploit the region's rich mineral deposits. Peter even transformed the way Russians looked—he ordered his courtiers to wear western clothes, and nobles to shave off their traditional Russian beards. Any one who refused had to pay a tax.

Peter's programs were aimed at making Russia competitive with the west. He did not attempt to reform Russia's deeply conservative society, and introduced repressive measures of control such as censorship of the press. Serfs were subjected to new restrictions, taxed heavily to pay for Peter's schemes, and forced to work on the construction of St. Petersburg; thousands died in terrible conditions. Serfdom was even extended to industrial workers in Peter's newly built factories.

## MIGHTY RUSSIA

During the 18th century, Russian's frontiers expanded slowly. The Ottoman Turks were driven from the Crimea and southern Ukraine, and with the fall of Sevastopol in 1783 the Black Sea was opened to Russian trade. Russian fur traders crossed the Bering Sea to North America and founded the first permanent European settlements in Alaska in 1784. But the most significant gain was on its western frontier, where Russia benefited from Poland's weakness to share with Austria and Prussia in the partition of the kingdom between 1772 and 1795. At the end of the Napoleonic wars (see pages 36–39), the Congress of Vienna (1815) ceded the rest of Poland to Russia.

Many of these territorial gains were made in the reign of the German-born empress Catherine the Great (1762–96), who came to the throne upon the death of her highly unpopular husband, Peter III, grandson of Peter the Great. Catherine was suspected by many of being implicated in his murder, and she has won great notoriety for her love affairs. However, she ruled Russia firmly

## SAINT PETERSBURG

*Peter the Great chose a marshy site on the Neva river, at the head of the Gulf of Finland, to be his "window on Europe." He laid the foundations for the Peter-Paul Fortress in May 1703, and in 1712 the city became his capital. A wave of building followed, all according to an elegant plan centered on Peter's vast Admiralty building and shipyards. Later rulers added to its splendors with new buildings in a variety of baroque and neoclassical styles, among them the magnificent Winter Palace (now the Hermitage). Known as Leningrad during the period of Soviet rule, the city's original name was restored in 1991.*

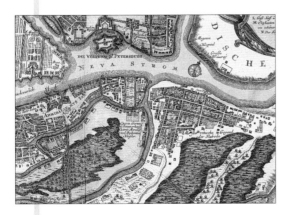

**Above** *A map of St. Petersburg in 1728.*
**Right** *View from the river about the same time.*

and well. An autocrat, she was also keenly interested in the cultural movements of the day in art, music, and architecture. Her collection of paintings forms the core of the great national collection now in the Hermitage Museum in St. Petersburg. At her invitation, many Germans settled in Russia, particularly in the newly conquered areas north of the Black Sea, where they introduced efficient agriculture.

In common with her fellow European monarchs, Catherine was alarmed by the outbreak of the French revolution in 1789. As the revolutionaries tried to spread their ideas across Europe, Russia joined Austria, Spain, Prussia and Britain in the war against France (see pages 36–39). Catherine was succeeded by her son Paul in 1796, but his erratic policies (he sent a Cossack army to conquer India) led to his murder in 1801. His son Alexander I attacked Sweden to take possession of Finland (1808). In 1812 Napoleon invaded Russia but was defeated by its unmanageable size. As the French retreated, Alexander placed himself at the head of the pursuing Russian army, and entered Paris with the allies in 1814. Russia was now established as one of the great powers of Europe.

*Above* Catherine the Great, whose expansionist foreign policy brought new gains to Russia.

# THE MUSLIM WORLD

BETWEEN 1500 AND 1800, ASIA WAS DOMINATED BY THREE GREAT ISLAMIC STATES: THE OTTOMAN IN THE MIDDLE EAST AND THE BALKANS, THE SAFAVID IN PERSIA, AND THE MUGHAL IN INDIA. ALL THREE HAD AMBITIONS TO ESTABLISH AN ISLAMIC WORLD EMPIRE AND WERE CONTINUALLY PUSHING TO EXPAND THEIR BOUNDARIES OUTWARDS. AT THE SAME TIME, THEY ARGUED AMONG THEMSELVES OVER CLAIMS TO GOVERN THE MUSLIM WORLD.

*Left* Ottoman sea power struck at the heart of Venice's maritime empire. The defeat of the Ottoman navy at the battle of Lepanto (1571) marked a revival in European fortunes, but the eastern Mediterranean remained a closed Ottoman lake for another century.

At the beginning of the 16th century the Ottomans were the most powerful Muslim dynasty. In the 14th century, as the Byzantine empire declined, they had expanded from their base in Anatolia (Turkey) to conquer Bulgaria, Greece, and Serbia. Edirne (formerly Adrianople), 140 miles northwest of the Byzantine capital, was their center of government until Constantinople itself fell to the armies of Mehmet II in 1453. The ancient capital of the eastern Roman empire and the seat of the Orthodox patriarch now became the capital of the Ottoman sultans and the administrative center of their highly organized empire. The church of St. Sophia was converted to a mosque.

The Balkan parts of the empire were crucially important to its success. The sultan's Christian subjects had to send a tribute of children to Constantinople each year (the *devshirme*). Here, they were brought up as Muslims and educated to serve in the government or fight in the highly trained elite corps of Janissaries, the sultan's personal guard. Although slaves, the Janissaries were well treated and could rise to high positions of wealth and authority in the empire. Constantinople at this time was a more cosmopolitan and tolerant city than most European capitals; many of its citizens were Greek Christians and Jews.

Selim I (r.1512–20) was the most successful of the Ottoman sultans; during his reign, Syria and Kurdistan were conquered from the Safavids and the holy city of Mecca taken into Ottoman control. His successor,

Suleiman the Magnificent (r.1520–66), added Hungary, Iraq, and the North African coast. Expansion started to slow from then on: long supply lines hindered military campaigns. The authority of the sultans began to weaken, and the Janissaries, who had developed into a hereditary privileged class that meddled in politics, ceased to be a powerful fighting force.

The Muslim empires no longer dominated trade with India and the Far East. The British and Dutch controlled the Indian Ocean trade, while the opening up of Siberia had created a land route to China that bypassed Ottoman and Safavid territories. The Ottomans were in economic and military decline. In 1683 a last great campaign in Europe ended in crushing defeat at the gates of Vienna. Hungary was won back by Austria in 1699. Further losses followed, and by 1800 the draining away of territory in the Balkans, and in North Africa, had become a steady and irreversible process.

Ottoman empire, 1512

gains under Selim I and Suleiman I, 1512–1566

gains 1566–1683

Ottoman empire, 1815

Safavid empire, 1722

Ottoman territory effectively independent by 1815

Ottoman administrative center

Ottoman campaign

borders, 1815

0                    800 km
0                    600 mi

PRUSSIA

RUSSIA

BELARUS

*Volga*

Kazan

Moscow

Cossacks

POLAND

*Dnieper*

Kiev

1521

Cossacks

Krakow

1502, 1519

UKRAINE

1527, 1543

Astrakhan

AUSTRIAN EMPIRE

1529

Jedisan

Azov

1531

Buda

Jassy

Bessarabia

Khanate of the Crimea
1774–83 independent

1579–80

Derbent

*Caspian*

1532

Hungary

Transylvania

Moldavia

1538

Akkerman

CAUCASUS MTS.

Daghestan

Baku

TURKMENISTAN

Mohács

ROMANIA

Kaffa

Georgia

Tiflis

*Karabagh*

Belgrade

1526

Wallachia

Bucharest

*Danube*

Silistria

Black Sea

Batum

Yerevan

Kars

Bosnia

Sarajevo

Nish

Bulgaria

Varna

Amasra

Sinope

Trabzon

Chaldiran
1514

Tabriz

Serbia

Sofia

1526

Edirne
(Adrianople)

Armenia

HERAT

Ragusa

MONTENEGRO

Constantinople

Ankara

Sivas

Kurdistan

Azerbaijan

ZAGROS

Tehran

Taranto

Rumelia

Bursa

ANATOLIA

Mardin

Mosul

Hamadan

Qum

SAFAVID
EMPIRE

Gallipoli

OTTOMAN
EMPIRE

Kayseri

Urfa

MTS.

Reggio

Albania

GREECE

TURKEY

Konya

Adana

Qasr-i-
Shirin

Isfahan

IRAN

Lepanto
1571

Morea

Athens

Izmir

Aleppo

*Euphrates*

*Tigris*

Luristan

1543

*Rhodes*

Syria

Baghdad

Iraq

PERSIA

CANDIA

Crete

Cyprus

Tripoli

1574

Damascus

1551

*Mediterranean Sea*

Jerusalem

Basra

1554

Benghazi

CYRENAICA
semi-independent 1714

Alexandria

Damietta

Arabs

El Hasa

Bandar Abbas

Hormuz

TRIPOLI
semi-independent
1714

Cairo

Suez

BAHRAIN
independent 1783

1521

QATAR
independent
1780

LIBYA

EGYPT
semi-independent
1805

Asyut

Quseir

*Hejaz*

Muscat

OMAN
independent 1650

El Kharga

SAUDI ARABIA

OMAN

## THE SAFAVID EMPIRE

Safavid Persia, on the Ottoman empire's eastern border, was established by
Shah Ismail I (r.1501–24) who expanded from a power base in Azerbaijan to
occupy the area between the Caspian
Sea and the Persian Gulf. This growth
was abruptly halted when his army was
defeated by the Ottomans at the battle of
Chaldiran in 1514. The Ottomans continued to make inroads into Safavid territory
until Shah Abbas the Great (r.1588–1629)
revived the Safavid fortunes. After strength-
ening the army by replacing the old military
elite with a slave caste of Muslim converts
similar to the Ottoman corps of Janissaries,
he won back most of the land in western
Persia lost to the Ottomans and captured
Kandahar (Afghanistan) from the Mughals

Medina

*Red Sea*

*Nile*

Selima

Jiddah

**Mecca**

Suakin

*Right* Suleiman the
Magnificent was
painted by the Venetian
artist Titian. He was
known to the Turks as
the "Law Giver."

SUDAN

Massawa

Sana

YEMEN
independent
1635

YEMEN

FUNJ

Mocha

Aden

ETHIOPIA

of northern India. Abbas made Isfahan the Persian capital in 1587, which he adorned with many mosques. Persian poetry, painting, and architecture flourished under his rule. He was followed by a succession of mediocre rulers, but the Safavid empire survived until 1722 when it was overrun by Afghan raiders. Persia briefly revived during the reign of Nadir Shah (1736–47), a bandit turned general who conquered Afghanistan and raided Delhi in 1739.

## THE MUGHALS

Muslim invaders from Afghanistan had established the first Islamic state in India in the 11th century. By the 14th century the sultanate of Delhi ruled most of northern India and had extended its control far into central India (the Deccan), but it was in decline when the Mughals—a central Asian dynasty claiming descent from the Mongols—invaded India under Babur (r.1501–30) in 1519. After defeating the sultanate of Delhi at the first battle of Panipat (1526), he went on to conquer most of northern India. Rebellions broke out after his death but his grandson Akbar (r.1556–1605) took Mughal rule into the Deccan.

Akbar was a competent and wise ruler. Although a devout Muslim, he encouraged religious toleration among his Hindu subjects for the sake of stability. His empire was prosperous. Its grain harvests were larger than all of Europe's together, it possessed the world's largest textile industry, and produced high-quality steel and cannon. The weapons employed by the Mughals' professional army of a million soldiers were the equal of any used in the west at that time.

The Mughal empire was at its greatest under Aurangzeb (r.1658–1707), who conquered all but the far south of India. By now, Mughal rule had become less tolerant, and Aurangzeb asserted his Islamic faith by destroying Hindu temples and holy places.

*Above* The Taj Mahal, the garden tomb built by the Mughal Shah Jahan for his favorite wife, 1632–54.

From the mid 17th century resistance to Mughal rule was headed by the Marathas, a military Hindu state based in the western Deccan. Mughal power declined after Aurangzeb's death, and the Marathas were able to drive them from the Deccan and attack the north. Meanwhile, Nadir Shah of Persia took advantage of their weakness to sack Delhi in 1739. In a humiliating gesture, he took away the Peacock Throne of the Mughal emperors. Provincial governors began to rule like independent princes.

The opening up of trade with the west had led a number of European nations to establish trading bases on the Indian coast. The Mughals had welcomed the influx of European money to pay for their exports of spices, silk, cotton, and dyes, but the European trading companies now took advantage of Mughal weakness to increase their influence. Wars in Europe spilled over into colonial possessions. The Seven Years War (1756–63) greatly strengthened the position of the British East India Company. It possessed its own army and heavily armed ships and was able to intimidate and neutralize Indian opposition through a network of favorable alliances. By 1765 the British had won control of the rich Bengal cotton trade; by 1815 they dominated India and the Mughal emperor was a mere puppet.

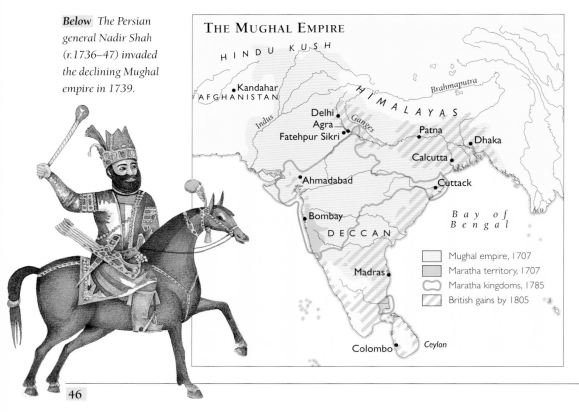

*Below* The Persian general Nadir Shah (r.1736–47) invaded the declining Mughal empire in 1739.

### THE MUGHAL EMPIRE

HINDU KUSH

Kandahar
AFGHANISTAN
Indus

HIMALAYAS

Brahmaputra

Delhi
Agra
Fatehpur Sikri
Ganges
Patna
Dhaka
Calcutta

Ahmadabad
Cuttack

Bombay

DECCAN

*Bay of Bengal*

Madras

Colombo
*Ceylon*

- Mughal empire, 1707
- Maratha territory, 1707
- Maratha kingdoms, 1785
- British gains by 1805

# THE ART OF MUGHAL INDIA

Mughal emperors were rich patrons of the arts, and they encouraged artists from Safavid Persia to their court, where they set up royal workshops. Persian artists excelled in creating books lavishly illustrated with miniature drawings and paintings in a formal, highly decorated style, which made brilliant use of color. Indian artists, Hindu and Muslim, were trained in the Mughal studios, and while they continued to work in the Persian style, they added to it a distinctly Indian view of life. Mughal art is especially noted for its delicate portraiture and its natural history paintings—two subjects largely ignored by the Safavids.

Under the patronage of the emperor Jahangir (r.1605–27), Mughal painting reached its richest expression. He prized individuality above all things, and rewarded one exceptional artist, the nature specialist Abu'l Hasan, with the title "Wonder of the Age."

Architecture and landscaping were also highly prized by the Mughals. The first emperor, Babur, was an avid maker of gardens—an interest he brought to India from Central Asia. The emperor who has left the greatest architectural legacy is Shah Jahan (r.1628–66). He oversaw the construction of the Peacock Throne, rebuilt Lahore and Agra, laid out a new capital at Delhi, and built the Taj Mahal as a tomb for his favorite wife.

**Below** *Shah Jahan on the Peacock Throne.*

# IMPERIAL CHINA

CHINA HAS ALWAYS BEEN OPEN TO INVASION FROM THE NORTH. THE MING DYNASTY, WHO EXPELLED THE MONGOLS AND RULED CHINA FROM 1368–1644, BUILT THE 2,000-MILE-LONG GREAT WALL TO PROTECT THIS VULNERABLE FRONTIER. BUT IT PROVED A FAILURE. DURING A CIVIL WAR IN 1644, MANCHU TRIBESMEN FROM THE NORTH WERE ABLE TO INVADE THE EMPIRE AND CAPTURE BEIJING. AS THE QING DYNASTY, THEY WERE TO BE THE LAST RULERS OF IMPERIAL CHINA.

Under the Ming emperors, China began a period of stable government. Chinese rule extended farther than ever before, into Vietnam and Burma in the south and Mongolia and Korea in the north. But Ming China was inward looking. Early in the 15th century, the admiral Zheng He sailed as far as east Africa, but maritime expeditions ended with his death in 1433. The decision to move the capital back to Beijing from the thriving ports of the south reflected the lack of enthusiasm for overseas trade. A Portuguese trading base was founded at Macau in 1557, and a Dutch settlement on Taiwan in 1622, but Ming relations with European merchants remained distant.

## THE MANCHUS IN POWER

By the early 17th century Ming authority had begun to crumble. Liaodong, the Chinese enclave north of the Wall, was protected by a wooden defensework with gate towers (the Willow Palisade) but this did not prevent it being seized by a new rival power, the Manchus, Jürchen tribesmen from the north. When civil war broke out in China, the Manchus stepped in. Dorgun (r. 1628–50) won control of Beijing in 1644 and acted as regent to his nephew who was installed as the first Qing emperor. It took several years to bring southern China under control: Manchu rule was never popular

*Below A vase of the Ming period. At this time, the secret of making porcelain was unknown in Europe, where there was a huge demand for quality items such as this. Many articles were produced in China especially for the export market.*

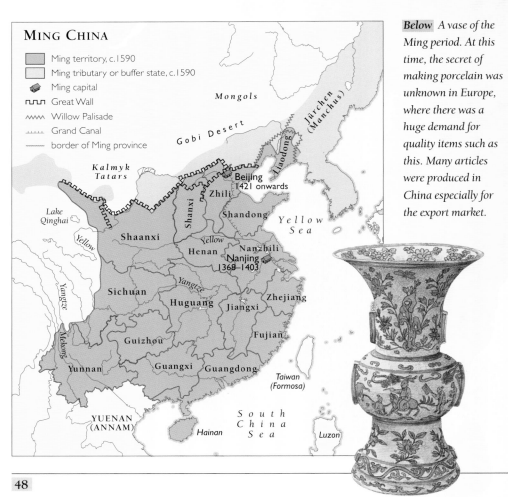

### MING CHINA

- ⬛ Ming territory, c.1590
- ⬜ Ming tributary or buffer state, c.1590
- 🏯 Ming capital
- ⅏ Great Wall
- ᗯᗯ Willow Palisade
- ⁙⁙⁙ Grand Canal
- — border of Ming province

### (Manchu map legend)

- ⬛ Manchu homeland, early 17th century
- ⬛ Manchu expansion to 1644
- ⬜ Manchu expansion, 1644–1697
- ⬜ Manchu expansion, 1697–1800
- ⬜ state paying tribute to Manchu China at some time between 1637 and 1800
- 🏯 Manchu provincial capital
- — trade route of the Manchu empire
- **silk** commodity traded
- ▷ internal migration of Han Chinese during the 18th century
- ═══ borders, c.1800
- ⅏ Great Wall
- ᗯᗯ Willow Palisade
- ⁙⁙⁙ Grand Canal

0 ———————— 1000 km
0 ———————— 800 mi

# 1644–1796

RUSSIAN EMPIRE

*Lake Baykal*

Kobdo

Uliastay

Kyakhta

**furs, gold, silver**
from Russia
**cotton fabrics, silk, tea**
to Russia

Ulan Bator

*Inner Mongolian Plateau*

Khalka

OUTER MONGOLIA

Setsen

Amur

*Amur*

Solon

Aigun

Mergen

Heilungjiang

Heje Kiakia

Qiqihar

MANCHURIA

Kurka

Khorchin

**ginseng, soya beans**
from Manchuria;
**cotton fabrics, tea**
to Manchuria

Jilin

Jürchen
(Manchus)

Hunchun

*Sea of Japan*

*Kalmyk Tatars*

ni

*Tushiyetu*

*Gobi Desert*

Chahar

INNER MONGOLIA

Kalgan

*Songhua*

Shenyang
(Mukden)

Niuzhuang

Liaodong

Wonsan

KOREA

JAPAN

Anxi

territory added
to Gansu 1759

Suzhou

Ganzhou

*Alashan Eleuth*

*Ordos Desert*

Ningxia

Beijing

Jinzhou

Seoul

Pusan

*QILIAN MTS*

Qinghai

*Lake Qinghai*

Lanzhou

Gansu

Taiyuan

Shanxi

Zhili

Ji'nan

Shandong

Dengzhou

*Yellow Sea*

*Yellow*

*QIN MTS*

Shaanxi

Xi'an
(Chang'an)

Kaifeng

Henan

Huai'an

Jiangsu

**copper**
from Japan;
**medicines, silk, sugar**
to Japan

*Han*

*Yellow*

*DABA MTS*

Wushan

Hubei

Wuchang

Hefei

Anhui

Nanjing

Hangzhou

Mingzhou

*East China Sea*

Chamdo

Sichuan

Chengdu

*Yangtze*

*Lake Dongting*

*Lake Pengli*

Zhejiang

Wenzhou

*Salween*

*Yalong*

Chongqing

Nanchang

AM

Tanzhou

Hunan

Jiangxi

**copper**
from Japan

Guizhou

Guiyang

Fuzhou

Fujian

*Mekong*

Dali

Yunnan

Guilin
(Guizhou)

Ganzhou

Xiamen
(Amoy)

*Taiwan (Formosa)*

Yunnan

Guangdong

*Irrawaddy*

MIAN

Ava

*Salween*

Guangxi

*Xi*

Guangzhou
(Canton)

Fort Zeelandia
1624–62 to the
Netherlands

YANMAR

Tongking

Macau
to Portugal

*South China Sea*

Thang Long
(Hanoi)

Qiongzhou

Lan Chang
(Luangprabang)

LAOS

*Hainan*

gu

Rangoon

Vien Chan
(Vientiane)

SIAM

*THAILAND*

ANNAM

VIETNAM

**opium, silver**
from India;
**raw cotton, rice, woods**
from southeast Asia;
**cotton fabrics, ironware, porcelain, silk**
to southeast Asia;
**porcelain, silk, tea**
to Europe

*Tonle Sap*

CAMBODIA

Cochin China

***Above*** *The Great Wall across northern China.*

49

there. Once firmly established in power, the Qing set about the conquest of Mongolia, Turkestan, and Tibet. Qing expansionism made China a greater territorial power in east Asia than at any previous period in its history. Neighboring states such as Ladakh, Nepal, Bhutan, Laos, Burma, and Annam (Vietnam) were forced to make regular payments of tribute. Military protectorates in the northeast ended Russian expansion into Central Asia.

## STABILITY & GROWTH

After a five-year uprising was put down in 1681, China enjoyed more than a century of peace and stability under Qing rule. The most obvious change they introduced was the custom of wearing the hair in a queue, or single braid, in the traditional Manchu style; they showed their authority by making their Chinese (Han) subjects wear the same. Manchus were not allowed to marry Chinese. The only occupations open to them were the army and civil service.

The Manchus brought new efficiency to Chinese military and political life, but did not attempt to reform the thousand-year-old system of administration. In all but

the most senior posts, civil servants and soldiers continued to be drawn from the landowning class, who were recruited for their knowledge of ancient Chinese classics rather than their demonstration of practical skills. Peasant revolts during the late Ming period had virtually ended serfdom, but millions of tenant farmers lived at subsistence level. They could not afford the education to enter the imperial bureaucracy, but carried most of the tax burden.

Between 1650 and 1800 the population rose from 100 million to 300 million. The agricultural heartlands of the Yangtze basin and southeast were by now overpopulated, and this forced large numbers of peasants to migrate. The Qing forbade Han Chinese to settle in the Manchu homelands north of the Great Wall, so movement was principally to the less crowded western provinces.

## WIDER CONTACTS

While the Qing pursued their expansionist policies in Asia, they showed as little interest in trading on equal terms with Europe as their Ming predecessors had. As long as the Chinese economy was self-

*Left* The emperor Qianlong (r.1735–96) had the longest reign in Chinese history. Highly educated and a patron of the arts, he regarded China as the only powerful and civilized country in the world. He declined the innovations of the west, while appreciating its technical skills.

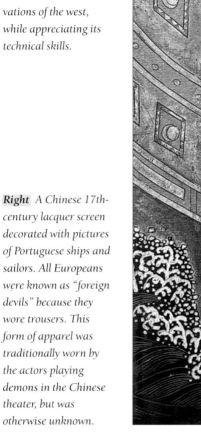

*Right* A Chinese 17th-century lacquer screen decorated with pictures of Portuguese ships and sailors. All Europeans were known as "foreign devils" because they wore trousers. This form of apparel was traditionally worn by the actors playing demons in the Chinese theater, but was otherwise unknown.

## BEIJING: NORTHERN CAPITAL

Beijing had been a frontier town for centuries before the Mongol leader, Kublai Khan, founder of the Yuan dynasty, made it his capital in 1267 and gave it its present name, which means "northern capital." It has remained China's capital ever since, with two brief interruptions when Nanjing was used: from 1368–1421 by the Ming; and from 1929–49 by the nationalist Kuomintang government.

The buildings seen today were mostly constructed under the Ming and Qing. As the capital grew under the Ming, they built

*Left* A lion guards the Forbidden City, Beijing.

sufficient and bolstered by the payment of tribute from its weaker neighbors, it had little incentive to trade abroad. China was the world's most advanced civilization; westerners were regarded as barbarians who had nothing to offer by way of material goods or technological knowledge, though there was a thriving trade in furs from Russia through the Mongolian trading city of Kyakhta.

Seventeenth-century Europe saw a growing fashion for all things Chinese, particularly porcelain, cotton, silks, and tea. As European traders had nothing the Chinese wanted to buy, they paid for their exports with New World silver, which proved very expensive. All European trade was restricted to the port of Guangzhou (Canton) in the south. Jesuit priests were also active in China during the 17th century. They were tolerated for their knowledge of physics and astronomy—though these were considered amusing trifles—but won few converts. Christianity was later banned because it conflicted with ancestor worship.

## CHINA'S SWIFT DECLINE

In 1793, the emperor Qianlong (r.1735–96) snubbed a British trade delegation. Its leader, Lord Macartney, had refused to prostrate himself in the traditional kowtow, or deferential bow, to the emperor, but this was probably just a pretext for breaking off relations. Notes taken by the delegation of Chinese methods of silk and tea production were passed to the British East India Company, which quickly set up in competition to the Chinese. At the end of Qianlong's reign there were obvious signs of Chinese decline. The civil service had become corrupt, and tax increases provoked a new wave of peasant rebellions. European technological superiority was becoming obvious even to the Qing court, but it was too conservative to contemplate modernization. By the mid 19th century, as China came closer to collapse, the west was able to impose its own terms for trade.

*a new wall to enclose Kublai Khan's original walled city. Imposing gates marked the entrance at each wall. The new outer city became Beijing's thriving commercial and residential district, while the old inner city of the Mongols became the Imperial City, the heart of the Chinese bureaucracy. Within the Imperial City, behind yet another wall, lay the Forbidden City, the compound of private palaces and gardens where the imperial family lived. Beijing escaped destruction in the wars of the early 20th century, and today the Forbidden City, which is not used by the Communist government, is open to the public as a museum.*

*Right Fishermen using cormorants for catching fish on the Yangtze river.*

# THE EMERGENCE OF AFRICA

ALTHOUGH THE ARRIVAL OF EUROPEAN TRADERS HAD GROWING CONSEQUENCES FOR AFRICAN SOCIETIES AND CULTURE IN THE CENTURIES AFTER 1500, THEIR INFLUENCE DID NOT EXTEND EVERYWHERE IN THE CONTINENT AND SEVERAL IMPORTANT INDIGENOUS AFRICAN STATES EMERGED DURING THIS PERIOD. ELSEWHERE, THE MASS TRANSPORTATION OF AFRICANS TO THE AMERICAS, IN CONDITIONS OF GREAT CRUELTY, HAD DEVASTATING IMPACT. BY THE TIME THE SLAVE TRADE WAS ABOLISHED IN THE 1800s, SOME 10–15 MILLION PEOPLE HAD BEEN SHIPPED FROM AFRICA TO PLANTATIONS IN THE NEW WORLD.

*Left  An ivory mask from the west African state of Benin.*

Trade in gold and ivory, rather than conquest, was the aim of the Portuguese who first began to build fortified bases around the African coast in the late 15th century. Soon slaves were also being traded from Africa and exported as forced labor to the plantations of Brazil and the Caribbean (see pages 16–19). Dutch, English, and French traders founded trading bases alongside the Portuguese, attracted by the profitable trade in human lives. Their arrival had considerable impact in some areas, disrupting existing patterns of trade and cultural exchange. The creation of new coastal networks for trade in west Africa drew commerce away from the wealthy trading kingdoms of the upper Niger. The powerful Songhai empire, which controlled the trade routes across the western Sahara, began to decline in the 16th century and was overthrown by a Moroccan army in 1591, which established a governorship in the region. The successor states of Segu and Kaarta were never able to match Songhai's former influence.

A number of small states, such as the Mossi, Oyo, and Benin, emerged in equatorial west Africa during the 16th and 17th centuries. Asante and Dahomey, dominating the coast, had become powerful and well-organized centralized kingdoms by the late 18th century, partly as a result of their involvement in the the slave trade.

South of the Equator, Portuguese traders exploited rivalry between the kingdoms of Congo and Ndongo to establish a colony at Luanda (Angola) by 1575. Njinga, queen of the Ndongo (r.1624–63), fought a long war to stop Portuguese slavers from extending their activities, but was forced to submit.

The Portuguese founded a string of bases on the east coast of Africa to dominate the Indian Ocean trade. Their presence upset the existing balance of power. Mwenemutapa, the most powerful state of southern Africa in the 16th century, asked the Portuguese for help in suppressing a rebellion, but found itself unable to resist their extortionate demands for trade and mining privileges. By the 1630s it had become a puppet state, and was later eclipsed by the neighboring kingdom of Rozwi.

## ISLAMIC STATES

Many parts of Africa were unaffected by the presence of European traders, and several important African states emerged at this time that owed nothing to their influence. Kanem-Bornu, on the southern edge of the Sahara, was the leading Islamic state in Africa and built up its power by importing firearms from the Ottomans. Farther to

*Below  A camel caravan crosses the western Sahara from Morocco. By the 16th century this route was declining in importance.*

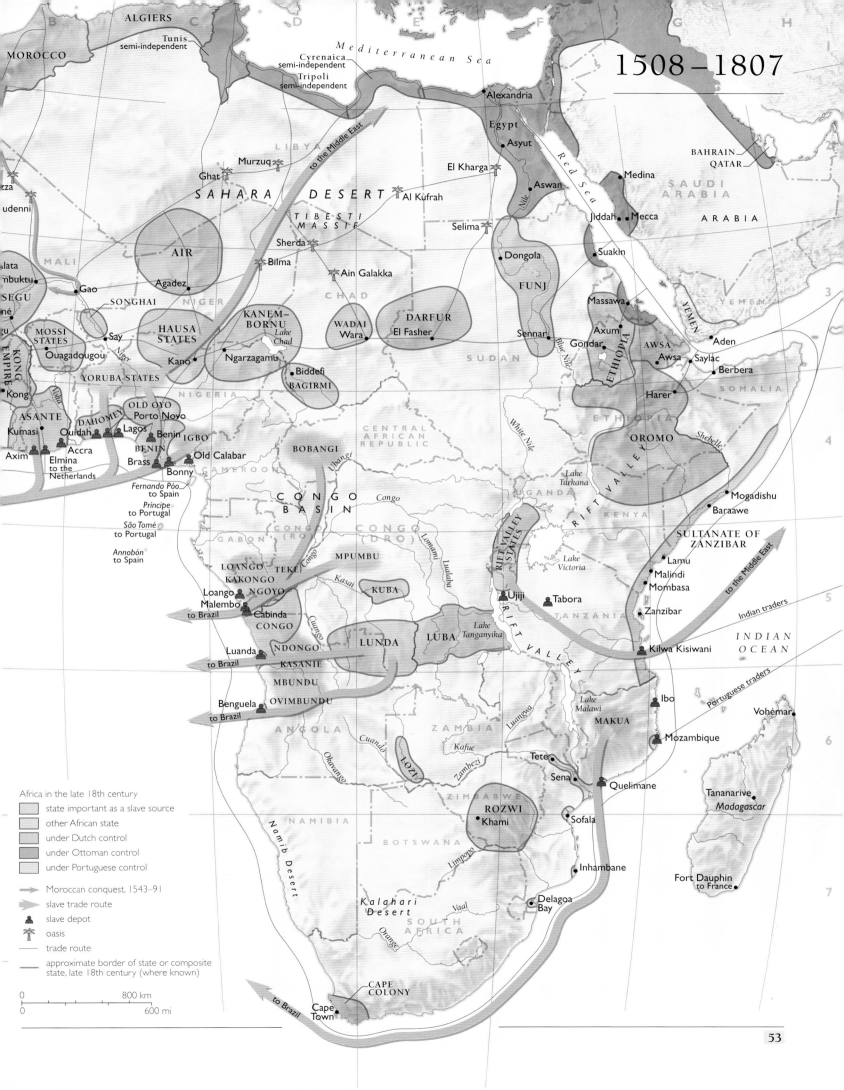

# 1508–1807

**MOROCCO**

ALGIERS

Tunis
semi-independent

Cyrenaica
semi-independent

Tripoli
semi-independent

*Mediterranean Sea*

Alexandria

Egypt

Asyut

El Kharga

Aswan

*Red Sea*

BAHRAIN
QATAR

Medina

SAUDI
ARABIA

ARABIA

*L I B Y A*

Murzuq

Ghat

S A H A R A      D E S E R T

Al Kufrah

*T I B E S T I
MASSIF*

Selima

Jiddah   Mecca

Suakin

AIR

Sherda

Bilma

Ain Galakka

Dongola

FUNJ

Massawa

ARABIA

*Izza*

*udenni*

Agadez

NIGER

*C H A D*

Axum

AWSA

*YEMEN*

Aden

Awsa
Saylac

*Wata*

*mbuktu*

Gao

SEGU

*né*

SONGHAI

HAUSA
STATES

KANEM-
BORNU

*Lake
Chad*

WADAI
Wara

DARFUR
El Fasher

*S U D A N*

Sennar

Gondar

ETHIOPIA

Berbera

SOMALIA

MOSSI
STATES

Say

Kano

Ngarzagamu

Harer

*u*

*KONG
EMPIRE*

Ouagadougou

Biddefi

BAGIRMI

*E T H I O P I A*

OROMO

*Shebelle*

Kong

YORUBA STATES

NIGERIA

*White Nile*

*Blue Nile*

*U G A N D A*

Mogadishu

Baraawe

ASANTE

Kumasi

OLD OYO
Porto Novo

DAHOMEY

Ouidah  Lagos

Benin

IGBO

*CENTRAL
AFRICAN
REPUBLIC*

BOBANGI

*Lake
Turkana*

*K E N Y A*

SULTANATE OF
ZANZIBAR

Axim

Accra

Elmina

BENIN
Brass

Old Calabar

*CAMEROON*

*Ubangi*

Lamu

Malindi

Mombasa

Elmina
to the
Netherlands

Bonny

*Fernando Póo
to Spain*

*Príncipe
to Portugal*

*São Tomé
to Portugal*

*Annobón
to Spain*

C O N G O
B A S I N

*GABON*

*CONGO
(ROC)*

*CONGO
(DRC)*

*Congo*

MPUMBU

*Lomani*

*Lualaba*

RIFT VALLEY
STATES

*Lake
Victoria*

Ujiji

Tabora

Zanzibar

*INDIAN
OCEAN*

*Indian traders*

LOANGO
KAKONGO
NGOYO

TEKE

*Kasai*

KUBA

*T A N Z A N I A*

Loango

Malembo

Cabinda

CONGO

*Cuango*

LUNDA

LUBA

*Lake
Tanganyika*

Kilwa Kisiwani

*Portuguese traders*

*to Brazil*

Luanda

NDONGO

KASANJE

*to Brazil*

MBUNDU

Benguela

OVIMBUNDU

*to Brazil*

*A N G O L A*

*Cuando*

*Kasai*

LOZI

*Kafue*

*Lake
Malawi*

MAKUA

Ibo

*Vohémar*

Mozambique

*Z A M B I A*

*Luangwa*

*Zambezi*

Tete

Sena

Quelimane

Tananarive

*Madagascar*

*N A M I B I A*

*Okavango*

*ZIMBABWE*

ROZWI
Khami

Sofala

*B O T S W A N A*

Inhambane

*Namib
Desert*

*Kalahari
Desert*

*Vaal*

*Orange*

*Limpopo*

Delagoa
Bay

*S O U T H
A F R I C A*

Fort Dauphin
to France

CAPE
COLONY

Cape
Town

*to Brazil*

## Africa in the late 18th century

- state important as a slave source
- other African state
- under Dutch control
- under Ottoman control
- under Portuguese control

→ Moroccan conquest, 1543–91

→ slave trade route

slave depot

oasis

trade route

approximate border of state or composite
state, late 18th century (where known)

0 ——— 800 km

0 ——— 600 mi

the east, Islam and Christianity came into direct conflict, mainly because of the survival of the ancient Christian kingdom of Ethiopia. Adal, an alliance of Islamic states in neighboring Somalia, attempted to conquer Ethiopia in 1527 under the leadership of Ahmed Gran, an *imam*, who declared the campaign a *jihad* (holy war). Fighting lasted until 1543, when a small Portuguese force came to Ethiopia's aid. The invasion was repelled, and Gran was killed in battle.

## RISE & FALL OF SLAVERY

In the early 1500s only about 2,000 slaves were annually exported out of Africa, but by 1680 this figure had risen to 10,000. At the peak of the trade, in the second half of the 18th century, as many as 100,000 men, women, and children were shipped to the Americas in a single year. By this time, British shipping and commercial interests controlled the slave trade into the Caribbean (slaves for Brazil were supplied by the Portuguese from Angola). Ships voyaged to west Africa from Bristol, Liverpool, and London to exchange firearms, textiles, liquor, and other goods for slaves before sailing on to the Caribbean. Here the slaves were sold for rum and molasses for the return

journey, or shipped on to North America, where they were exchanged for cargoes of tobacco, timber, and other raw materials. The entire round trip became known as the "Triangular Trade." The second stage, in which the human cargo from Africa was shipped across the Atlantic, was simply called the "Middle Passage."

The transatlantic slave trade, carried out in conditions of the utmost inhumanity, inflicted appalling human misery. It caused enormous social disruption in the worst exploited areas of west and central Africa. Europeans did not take part in slave raids themselves but bought them from African traders. A kingdom could become wealthy through slavery but could only meet the demand for ever more slaves by constant attacks on its neighbors. Sometimes rulers even sold some of their own people, such as criminals, into slavery.

Some people, such as the Quakers, were always opposed to slavery. During the 18th-century, opinion against it spread further

### THE TRIANGULAR SLAVE TRADE

→ British trade in the North Atlantic, 18th century

**iron** commodity traded

NORTH ATLANTIC OCEAN

Liverpool
Bristol

tobacco, timber, fish, furs

New York
Boston

NORTH AMERICA

fruit, mahogany, molasses, rum, sugar

Charleston

slaves, mahogany, molasses

iron, firearms, rum

firearms, textiles and manufactured goods

AFRICA

Kingston

Fort James

slaves, gold, pepper

Lagos
Brass

SOUTH AMERICA

SOUTH ATLANTIC OCEAN

*Right* Conditions on the Middle Passage were appalling. The slaves were chained and crammed in their hundreds below decks with barely enough room for them to lie down. Food and water were in short supply, and sanitation non-existent; many slaves died of disease before reaching the Americas. Most who survived could expect only brutal treatment and a short life on the plantations. This picture of captives on board a slaver was painted by an officer of a British anti-slavery patrol that intercepted the ship in 1840.

## THE ROYAL BRONZES OF BENIN

The forest societies around the Niger delta developed the technique of bronze casting between the late 12th and 14th centuries. The raw materials were bars of copper alloy imported from the interior. When the Portuguese came to the area in the 1480s, they brought brass bracelets as trade goods, which were melted down and recast. One of the most prolific centers of bronze casting was the court of Benin. Unique to Benin are highly crafted decorative plaques, which are thought to be imitations of illustrations in Portuguese books. They were fixed to the pillars of ceremonial buildings: a 17th-century Dutch traveler to the kingdom of Benin described the king's palace as having "wooden pillars encased in copper, where their victories are depicted."

*Above* Benin plaque of a Portuguese soldier.

with the development of libertarian ideals, but abolitionists faced enormous resistance from commercial interests. Participation in the slave trade was outlawed by Britain in 1807 and the United States in 1808. However, slave-owning was allowed in British colonies until 1833, French colonies until 1848, and in the United States until 1865. The Portuguese did not ban the slave trade in their colonies until the 1880s.

In 1787 British philanthropists bought an area of land on the west coast of Africa to found a settlement for freed and runaway slaves, which became the colony of Sierra Leone. In 1816 Liberia was founded in an region to the south as a colony for former slaves from the southern United States.

## THE FIRST COLONY

The largest concentration of Europeans in Africa, numbering some 15,000 by 1800, was at Cape Colony, in south Africa, founded in 1652 by the Dutch East India Company as a stopping point for its ships on the long voyage to the East Indies. It had a Mediterranean climate and good land, and soon grew into a thriving colony. As well as Dutch settlers, it attracted large numbers of French Huguenots. In 1814 it was ceded permanently to Britain by the Dutch.

## TIMETABLE

**1529**
Songhai empire dominates west Africa

**1531–32**
The Portuguese build fortresses at Sena and Tete on the Zambezi River

**1543**
Portuguese help the Ethiopians defeat a Muslim invasion by Ahmed Gran of Adal

**1570**
Idris III Aloma establishes Kanem-Bornu as the greatest power between the Nile and the Niger

**1575**
The Portuguese settlement of Angola begins at Luanda

**1591**
A Moroccan army overthrows the empire of Songhai

**1633**
Uprising by empire of Mwenemutapa against the Portuguese is suppressed

**1652**
Cape Town is founded by Dutchman Jan van Riebeeck

**1698**
The sultan of Oman establishes a sultanate at Zanzibar to dominate east African coastal trade

**1713**
British slave trade to Spanish America begins

**1724**
Dahomey grows in power as a partner of European slave traders

**1780**
Transatlantic slave trade at its peak

**1787**
British settle 400 freed slaves in Sierra Leone

**1795**
Great Britain seizes Cape Town from the Netherlands

**1808**
The United States bans further shipments of slaves from Africa

**1816**
The American Colonization Society begins the "Liberia Project" to provide a home for freed slaves

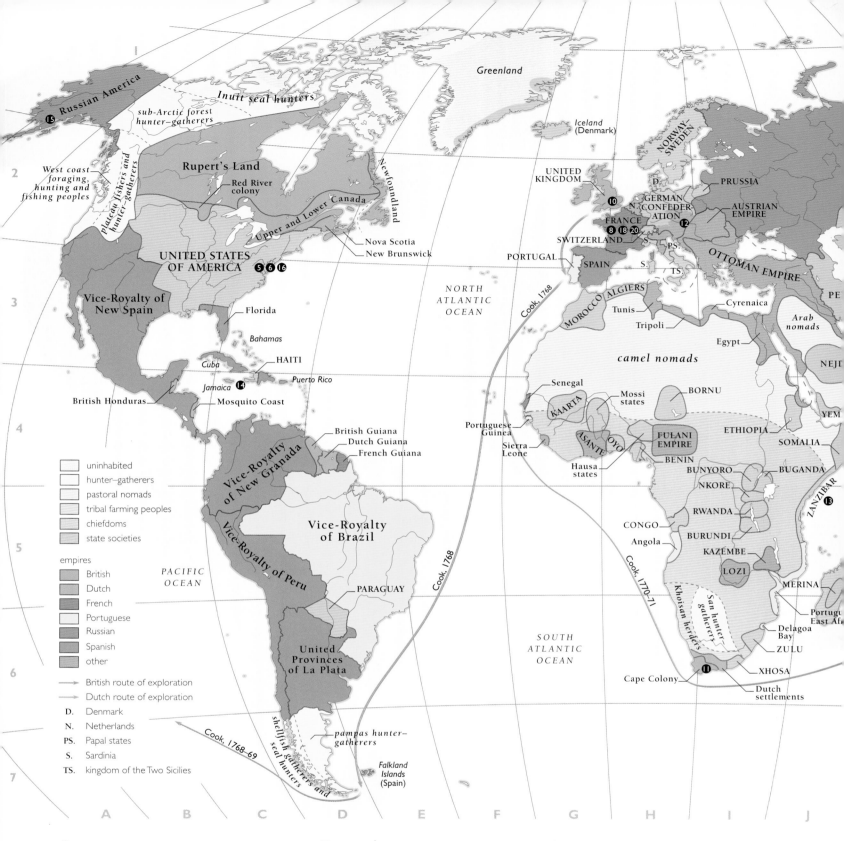

*Greenland*

Russian America

Inuit seal hunters

*sub-Arctic forest hunter–gatherers*

Iceland (Denmark)

⑮

NORWAY-SWEDEN

Rupert's Land

UNITED KINGDOM

PRUSSIA

*West coast foraging, hunting and fishing peoples*

Red River colony

⑩ GERMAN N. CONFEDERATION

AUSTRIAN EMPIRE

D.

*plateau fishers and hunter–gatherers*

Upper and Lower Canada

Newfoundland

FRANCE ⑫

⑧ ⑱ ⑳

SWITZERLAND S.

PS.

OTTOMAN EMPIRE

Nova Scotia
New Brunswick

UNITED STATES OF AMERICA

⑤ ⑥ ⑯

PORTUGAL

SPAIN S.

TS.

PE

Vice-Royalty of New Spain

Florida

NORTH ATLANTIC OCEAN

Cook, 1768

MOROCCO ALGIERS

Tunis

Cyrenaica

*Arab nomads*

Tripoli

Egypt

Bahamas

Cuba

HAITI

Puerto Rico

*camel nomads*

Senegal

BORNU

NEJI

British Honduras

Jamaica ⑭

Mosquito Coast

Portuguese Guinea

KAARTA

Mossi states

YEM

British Guiana
Dutch Guiana
French Guiana

Sierra Leone

ASANTE OYO

FULANI EMPIRE

ETHIOPIA

SOMALIA

Vice-Royalty of New Granada

Hausa states

BENIN

BUNYORO

BUGANDA

NKORE

uninhabited
hunter–gatherers
pastoral nomads
tribal farming peoples
chiefdoms
state societies

Vice-Royalty of Brazil

RWANDA

CONGO

BURUNDI

Angola

ZANZIBAR ⑬

KAZEMBE

Vice-Royalty of Peru

empires
British
Dutch
French
Portuguese
Russian
Spanish
other

PACIFIC OCEAN

PARAGUAY

LOZI

MERINA

Cook, 1768

Cook, 1770–71

*Khoisan herders*

*San hunter gatherers*

Portug East Af

Delagoa Bay

British route of exploration
Dutch route of exploration

D.     Denmark
N.     Netherlands
PS.   Papal states
S.     Sardinia
TS.   kingdom of the Two Sicilies

United Provinces of La Plata

SOUTH ATLANTIC OCEAN

ZULU

Cape Colony ⑪

XHOSA

Dutch settlements

Cook, 1768–69

*shellfish gatherers and seal hunters*

*pampas hunter–gatherers*

Falkland Islands (Spain)

A     B     C     D     E     F     G     H     I     J

❶ 1557  The Portuguese establish a trading base at Macau, China

❷ 1596  The first Dutch trading expedition reaches the East Indies

❸ 1603  The Tokugawa shogunate is established in Japan with its capital at Edo (Tokyo)

❹ 1615  The Manchus begin the conquest of the ailing Ming empire

❺ 1620  The Pilgrims land at Cape Cod, Massachusetts

❻ 1626  The Dutch found the colony of New Amsterdam (New York)

❼ 1632  Shah Jahan begins the Mughal conquest of the Deccan (central India)

❽ 1638  Birth of Louis XIV of France; he succeeds to the throne in 1643, at the age 5

❾ 1638  The Japanese close their ports to foreign traders

❿ 1649  King Charles I of England is found guilty of high treason and executed

⓫ 1652  Dutch settlers found a colony at the Cape of Good Hope, South Africa

⓬ 1683  An army led by John Sobieski, king of Poland, defeats the Ottomans outside Vienna

⓭ 1698  The Omanis drive the Portuguese from Mombasa and set up the Zanzibar sultanate

⓮ 1713  Britain takes over control of the African slave trade to the Caribbean from the Spanish

⓯ 1784  Russian fur traders found a settlement in Alaska

# THE WORLD BY 1815

**RUSSIAN EMPIRE**

Central Asian Khanates

MANCHU EMPIRE

Ainu hunter–gatherers

AFGHANISTAN

KOREA

JAPAN

NEPAL   BHUTAN

Indian princely states

India

BURMA

Taiwan

OMAN

LAOS

ARAKAN

ANNAM

SIAM

Goa

CAMBODIA

Philippine Islands

KANDY   Ceylon

COCHIN CHINA

ACEH

Malay states

Celebes

Borneo

Sumatra

Dutch East Indies

New Guinea

Papuan farmers

Solomon Islands

Melanesians

Java

Timor

Tasman, 1642–43

Mauritius (Britain)

Cook, 1770

INDIAN OCEAN

Australian Aboriginal hunter–gatherers

New South Wales

Cook, 1770

New Hebrides

Fiji Islands

Tasman, 1642–43

New Caledonia

Tasman, 1642–43

Van Diemen's Land

Cook, 1769–70

Bay of Islands

Polynesians

Cook, 1769

Maori chiefdoms

L   L   M   N   O   P

By 1815 the European Age of Discovery was coming to an end. Exploration of the Pacific had added Australia and Antarctica to the known world. However, while European colonization had had great impact in some places, much of the world was still unaware of or unaffected by Europe. China, the world's largest empire, had distanced itself from contact with the West.

In 1492, the year that Columbus landed in the New World, Europe had occupied a fairly inconsequential position on the world stage. China was far advanced in technological skills, and it was reaching heights of prosperity and stability under the Ming. Asia's Islamic empires controlled international trade. Europe was unable to match the military and naval strength of the Ottoman empire. Over the next three hundred years, the European pursuit of wealth and territory had established colonies in every continent of the world. Their empire-building had had enormous impact on indigenous populations: in the Americas, thousands had been killed by war and disease, or displaced from their traditional lands. Millions of Africans had been enslaved and shipped across the Atlantic to provide labor on European plantations.

However, in 1815, European power was by no means global. Colonial settlement in Australia and Africa was limited to small coastal areas; their vast interiors remained unexplored. Through its control of trade in east Africa, the sultanate of Oman had greater territorial influence in Africa than the combined

**16** <u>1776</u>   The American colonies declare their independence from Britain

**17** <u>1788</u>   Britain founds a penal colony at Port Jackson (now Sydney), Australia

**18** <u>1789</u>   The French Revolution begins

**19** <u>1796</u>   The emperor Qianlong abdicates in China in order not to rule longer than his grandfather

**20** <u>1815</u>   Napoleon is defeated at Waterloo; the Congress of Vienna redraws the map of Europe

*Right* A 19th-century European's impression of a Tasmanian Aborigine. Australia was the last frontier of European colonization.

presence of European traders. The Chinese empire, the most populous in the world, was greater in size than at any previous time in history and had extended its influence far into southeast Asia. Although the military strength of the Ottoman empire was in decline, it was still a major territorial power in the Middle East and southern Europe.

By 1815, however, Europeans controlled the sea routes that acted as arteries for trade between the continents. Western traders were no longer reliant on overland caravan routes and Islamic middlemen. Until the 19th century, European goods had little allure for Indian and Chinese merchants, so silver and gold from the New World was used to buy the spices, cottons, silks, and porcelain that were so highly valued in the west. To facilitate this trade, European traders—especially Portuguese, Dutch, and British—had established permanent bases in Asia. In time, in southeast Asia and India, native traders were forced out of business and the European trading companies became territorial powers in their own right. A new global economy had come into being, from which the nations of the west derived almost exclusive benefits.

## EUROPE

Rivalry between the colonizing European nations was fierce, and by the end of the 18th century, dynastic and trade wars had come to replace the religious conflicts that had divided post-Reformation Europe. The

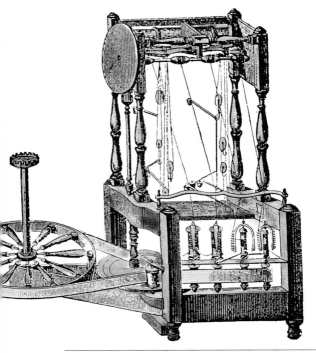

18th century saw a series of conflicts in Europe that spilled over into the colonies, especially North America. The French Revolution (1789) had plunged the continent into war, but Napoleon's defeat in 1815 saw a new balance of power emerging. The kingdom of Prussia was set to dominate European politics in the coming century. Russia, which had begun to modernize its feudal society in the early 18th century, continued to advance its borders in Asia and eastern Europe. Britain's naval strength and technical advances had made it the world's greatest manufacturing and trading power.

## THE AMERICAS

The rising power in the Americas was the United States. Since winning its independence from Britain in 1783 it had doubled in size with the purchase of Louisiana from France (1803). The War of 1812, fought over British restrictions on U.S. shipping, had heightened national pride and identity. As European settlers in the United States spread into the interior, Native Americans were pushed farther west into unsettled territory. In Central and South America, growing demands for independence, inspired by the American revolution and by Napoleon's occupation of Spain, had seen revolts break out against Spanish rule in Mexico (1810), Paraguay (1811), and Venezuela (1810–12). Haiti was the only island in the Caribbean to have won its independence, from France, after a slave revolt (1804).

## THE MIDDLE EAST

During the 18th century Ottoman power weakened in the Middle East and North Africa, with outlying states such as Tunis, Tripoli, Qatar, and Oman (which controlled trade with east Africa) declaring their independence. In Egypt, Mehmet Ali, an Albanian, succeeded in making himself viceroy in 1805. A dynamic, modernizing ruler, he helped to expel the fanatical Wahhabi sect from its control of the holy cities of Mecca and Medina, but became increasingly independent of the sultan. Despite signs of decline, however, the Ottoman empire was to survive for another century: it still controlled the Balkans from Greece to Romania, and Turkey, Syria, and Mesopotamia. Since the conquests of Nadir Shah's reign

*Left* Britain's early lead in the textile industry propelled it to a commanding position in the global economy. Mechanized production began to replace traditional handcrafting and Britain sought a larger market overseas for its manufactured goods. Seen here is Arkwright's spinning frame (1769).

**Above** With the establishment of overseas empires, wars between European powers took on a global aspect. In 1798 Napoleon invaded Egypt to try to cut off Britain's sea route to India, fast becoming its most important colony. His plan failed when the French fleet was defeated by the British in 1798 and its army was beaten in 1801.

(1736–47) Persia had become a cultural backwater and would find itself squeezed between the territorial ambitions of Russia in central Asia and British power in India.

## EAST & SOUTH ASIA

Under the Qing dynasty, China had made great territorial gains during the 18th century. The emperor Qianlong (r. 1736–96) had shunned the technical innovations of the west and successfully forced restrictions on foreign merchants, but his successors were unable to match his skills. Japan had deliberately closed its doors to European trade since the 17th century, and the mainland states of southeast Asia such as Burma and

Siam (Thailand) also resisted the incursions of the west. The Dutch had established a commercial empire in the spice islands of southeast Asia (the Dutch East Indies) in the 17th century, but by 1815 had lost their monopolies in the face of strong competition from British, French, American, and Chinese trade. The British had taken advantage of the decline of the Mughal empire in India to become the ruling power there.

## THE SOUTH PACIFIC

Parts of the Australian and New Zealand coastlines were first charted in the 17th century by Dutch mariners from the East Indies, but no attempt was made to settle

there until late in the 18th century, after Captain Cook, on his first Pacific voyage (1769–71), had claimed both for the British crown. The British government decided to found a convict colony in Australia: the first shiploads arrived in 1788. The Aboriginal population, which had inhabited Australia for at least 40,000 years, probably numbered around 300,000. European contact had catastrophic consequences. As many as 20,000 Aborigines may have been killed in early conflicts with settlers; others died in epidemics. As white settlement expanded, those living along the coasts were dispossessed of their lands and driven into the interior, where fierce intertribal conflicts developed. Their culture was destroyed.

# GLOSSARY

**abolitionist** A campaigner against slavery or the international slave trade.

**Aborigines** The earliest inhabitants of Australia, so called by Europeans because they had been there *ab origine*, "from the beginning."

**absolutism** A political system in which unrestricted power is exercised by a single ruler. It was practiced by many European monarchs in the 17th and 18th centuries. *See also* DIVINE RIGHT.

**Amerindian** One of any of the peoples who were in the Americas before the arrival of Europeans; a Native American.

**ancien régime** Meaning "old regime," the political and social system of France before the outbreak of the FRENCH REVOLUTION in 1789. More generally, it describes the ABSOLUTIST monarchies of 18th-century Europe.

**autocrat** A ruler who has unlimited authority. See ABSOLUTISM.

**Aztec** An AMERINDIAN empire that controlled Mexico and parts of central America before the Spanish conquest of 1519.

**baroque style** The art, architecture, and music of Europe in the 17th and 18th centuries. In architecture, it is marked by extravagant, flamboyant decoration and a dramatic sense of movement and contrast, and is found in ROMAN CATHOLIC churches in contrast to the severe interiors favored by PROTESTANTISM. See also COUNTER REFORMATION.

**Bastille** A medieval fortress in Paris that was used as a prison in the 18th century. It was stormed by a mob in July 1789, beginning the FRENCH REVOLUTION.

**Calvinism** A PROTESTANT doctrine founded by the French theologian John Calvin (1509–64) during the REFORMATION. It stresses the doctrine of predestination—that from eternity God predestines the salvation of a chosen elect.

**Code Napoleon** The law code compiled during the reign of the emperor Napoleon. It forms the basis of modern French law.

**Congress of Vienna** An international conference held in Vienna in 1814–15 to restore the balance of power in Europe after the defeat of Napoleon.

**conquistadors** The Spanish conquerors of the NEW WORLD.

**Constitution of the United States** The document embodying the fundamental principles upon which the law and federal system of government of the United States are based. It was drawn up at a convention of 55 delegates (the Constitutional Convention) who met at Philadelphia in 1787, and was ratified by the required number of states (nine) on June 21, 1788.

**Consul** A title (originally used in ancient Rome) adopted by Napoleon from 1799, when he became head of the French government, until 1804 when he made himself emperor.

**Cossacks** From the Turkic word *kazak*, meaning "adventurer" or "free man," peasants who fled from serfdom in Poland, Lithuania, and Russia to settle north of the Black Sea, where they enjoyed semi-independence. In the 17th and 18th centuries they came increasingly under Russian rule and revolted several times. They provided the elite cavalry regiments of the Russian army from the 18th to early 20th centuries.

**Counter Reformation** A movement of the ROMAN CATHOLIC church to halt the spread of the REFORMATION among PROTESTANTS in Europe and redefine the teachings of the church. To foster a new spirit of religious revival, orders such as the JESUITS were founded and new churches built in ornate BAROQUE STYLE. Missionaries were sent to win converts in Asia and the NEW WORLD.

**czar** The title of the ruler of Russia, derived from the ancient Roman imperial title of *caesar*. It was adopted by Ivan IV, grand prince of Moscow, in 1547 and used by his successors until the monarchy was abolished in 1917.

**divine right** The idea that monarchs are granted their power by God, so that disobedience to the king may be regarded as disobedience to the will of God. It was central to ABSOLUTISM.

**Dutch Republic** Known also as the United Provinces of the Netherlands, it consisted of the seven northern PROTESTANT provinces of the Netherlands that became independent of Spain (1558–1609). It became a major trading empire in the 17th century.

**East India Company** A company set up for the purpose of trading with east Asia. The Netherlands, England, and France all had national East India companies in the 16th and 17th centuries. They had their own armies for protection against European rivals and local resistance.

**Edict of Nantes** A proclamation of tolerance issued to French HUGUENOTS by Henry IV in 1598, ending the religious wars in France. It was revoked by Louis XIV in 1685, after which most Huguenots fled abroad.

**Enlightenment** An intellectual movement of 18th-century Europe that emphasized science and reason over religion and superstition.

**Estates-General** The French national assembly from the 14th to the late 18th centuries. It was organized on class lines: clergy (First Estate), nobility (Second Estate), and property-owning commoners (Third Estate). No assemblies were summoned between 1614 and 1789.

**Forbidden City** The residence of the Chinese emperor in Beijing.

**French and Indian War** A war fought in North America between France and Britain (1754–63), which resulted in France conceding all its territories in North America to Britain.

**French Revolution** The movement that saw the end of the ANCIEN RÉGIME in 1789 and convulsed France until 1799, when Napoleon overthrew the Revolutionary government.

**guillotine** A device for beheading people that became notorious in the FRENCH REVOLUTION, consisting of a weighted blade set between two upright posts.

**Habsburgs** A German dynasty who became counts of Austria in 1273, which they ruled without interruption, as archdukes and emperors, until 1918. In 1452 they acquired the title of Holy Roman emperor and retained it until the empire's dissolution in 1806. At the peak of Habsburg power in the 16th century, Charles V ruled the HOLY ROMAN EMPIRE, Spain, southern Italy, Burgundy, the Netherlands, Mexico, and Peru.

**hacienda** A large estate in the Spanish empire.

**Han** The ethnic majority of China.

**heresy** A religious belief that does not conform to church teaching.

**Holy Roman empire** The empire founded by Otto I in 962, based on his claim to be the legitimate successor of the western Roman emperors and the guardian of western Christianity. It controlled most of central Europe and northern Italy in the Middle Ages but slowly declined to become a loose confederation of semi-independent states. It was finally abolished by Napoleon in 1806.

**Huguenot** A French PROTESTANT of the 16th and 17th centuries.

**humanism** An intellectual movement of the RENAISSANCE that emphasized humanity's free will, superiority to nature, and relationship to God. It is summed up in the saying "Man (humanity) is the measure of all things." The leading proponent of humanism was the Dutch scholar Erasmus.

**Inca** An AMERINDIAN group that controlled an empire in the Andes and on the west coast of South America in the 15th century. It was conquered by Spain in 1535.

**indulgence** In ROMAN CATHOLICISM, the remission, or cancellation, of part or all of the eternal punishment due for sins that have been pardoned by an act of penance. The practice of selling indulgences without exacting penance was one of the church abuses that led to the REFORMATION.

**Industrial Revolution** The development of modern industry and factory production, with accompanying economic and social changes, that began in Britain in the 18th century and spread to the rest of Europe and North America.

**Inquisition** An organization of the ROMAN CATHOLIC church charged with identifying and punishing HERESY. It was most active in Spain.

**Jacobins** A radical political group that engaged in terrorist activities during the FRENCH REVOLUTION.

**Janissary** A member of a corps of slave-soldiers in the OTTOMAN empire, made up of Christian youths from the Balkan provinces. They converted to Islam on being drafted into the Ottoman service. The Janissaries gradually became an elite hereditary class with great political influence.

**Jesuit** A member of the Society of Jesus, a ROMAN CATHOLIC order founded by Ignatius Loyola in 1534. It was principally involved in missionary and education work.

**libertarian** A believer in freedom of expression and thought.

**Louisiana Purchase** An area of 828,000 square miles (2,144,520 sq km) lying between the Mississippi river and the Rocky Mountains, which was purchased for less than 3 cents an acre from France in 1803, doubling the size of the United States.

**Lutheranism** The branch of PROTESTANTISM that follows the principles of the German theologian Martin Luther (1483–1546).

**Mamluke** A dynasty of slave-soldiers, similar to the JANISSARIES, that ruled Egypt from 1250 to 1811.

**Manchu** A people from Manchuria in northeast Asia who invaded and conquered China in 1644, founding the QING dynasty, which ruled until 1911.

**Marathas** A Hindu people of west central India (the present state of Maharashtra) who created a warrior state in the 17th and 18th centuries.

**Ming** The ruling dynasty of China from 1368 to 1644. It was overthrown by the MANCHUS.

**Mughals** (also spelled Moguls) A Muslim dynasty that ruled a large part of India from the 16th to the 18th centuries. They were noted for their administrative efficiency and for their high level of cultural activity, especially in painting, textiles, and architecture.

**New World** The name given to the Americas by Europeans in the 16th century to distinguish them from the Old World of Europe, Asia, and Africa.

**Ninety-five Theses** An account of the failings of the ROMAN CATHOLIC church drawn up by Martin Luther in 1517. He nailed them to the door of the church in Wittenberg, an event that is held to mark the beginning of the REFORMATION.

**Ottoman** A Turkish dynasty that ruled an empire in the Middle East and southeast Europe between the 15th and early 20th centuries. Its capital was Constantinople, former capital of the Byzantine empire.

**Parliament** The legislative assembly of Great Britain, consisting of the sovereign, the House of Lords, and the House of Commons. The English parliament formed the center of opposition to the king in the English Civil War (1642–51).

**peon** A peasant laborer in Spain's American colonies.

**prime minister** From the 18th century, the senior minister of the British government.

**privateer** A pirate licensed by the government of one state to attack the ships of rival states.

**Protestantism** A religious movement that broke away from the the ROMAN CATHOLIC church in the 16th century REFORMATION. Its name is derived from the "Protestation" issued by a number of German princes in1529 against Charles V's refusal to allow the princes of the HOLY ROMAN EMPIRE to decide the religion of their own states. *See also* CALVINISM, LUTHERANISM.

**puppet state** A state that retains its own identity but is under the political control of another.

**Puritans** English PROTESTANTS of the 16th and 17th century who were followers of CALVINISM.

**Qing** The official name of the MANCHU dynasty that ruled China from 1644 to 1911.

**Reformation** The demand for reform of perceived abuses within the ROMAN CATHOLIC church that created a religious and political divide in western Europe during the 16th century, resulting in PROTESTANTISM.

**Renaissance** A cultural movement (literally meaning "rebirth") that began in Italy in the 14th century and had spread throughout Europe by the 16th century. A revival of interest in classical learning gave rise to a flowering in art, architecture, literature, philosophy, and science. *See also* HUMANISM.

**republic** A form of government in which elected representatives of the people have supreme power. The chief of state is not a hereditary monarch but an elected officer, usually a president (as in the United States).

**Roman Catholicism** The branch of Christianity that recognizes the supreme authority of the pope. It was the only church in western Europe until the REFORMATION.

**Romanov** The ruling dynasty of the Russian empire from 1613 to 1917.

**Romanticism** An artistic and intellectual movement of the late 18th to mid 19th centuries in Europe. It emphasized the beauty of nature and the value of emotion over reason.

**Safavid** The ruling dynasty of Persia (Iran) from 1502 to 1736.

**serfdom** A medieval institution in which peasant farmers were owned by their landlords and bound for life to the soil. It survived in parts of Europe until the 19th century.

**Seven Years War** A major European conflict (1756–63) in which France, Austria, Sweden, and Russia were aligned against Britain, Prussia, and Hanover. Much of the fighting took place in Europe's colonial empires: the North American phase of the war is known as the FRENCH AND INDIAN WAR. France lost most of its overseas empire to Britain. Prussia emerged as the major gainer in Europe.

**sultan** The ruler of a Muslim country, from the Arabic word meaning "rule."

**Tatars** (also spelled Tartars) A nomadic Turkic people of the south Russian steppes who were conquered by the Mongols in the 13th century and absorbed into the khanate of the Golden Horde, which dominated Russia until the late 15th century. As a result, the Mongols were frequently known as Tatars or Tartars.

**Treaty of Tordesillas** The agreement between Spain and Portugal in 1494 to divide the NEW WORLD.

# FURTHER READING

## GENERAL
Haywood, John, et al. *The Atlas of World History*. New York: M.E. Sharpe, 1997.
*The Oxford Atlas of Exploration*. New York: Oxford University Press, 1997.
Roberts, J.M., *A Concise History of the World*. New York: Oxford University Press, 1976.

## THE SPANISH–AMERICAN EMPIRE
Elliot, J. H. *The Hispanic World: Civilization and Empire*. London: Thames and Hudson, 1991.

## NORTH AMERICA
Daniel, C. (ed.) *Chronicle of America*. 2d ed. New York: DK Publishing, 1995.
Homberger, E. *Historical Atlas of North America*. New York: Penguin, 1995.
Middleton, Richard. *Colonial America: A History 1585–1776*. Malden, MA: Blackwell Publishers, 1996.
Tindall, George B., and Shi, David E. *America: A Narrative History*. New York: W.W. Norton and Co., 1996.

## EUROPE
Furet, François. *The French Revolution*. Malden, MA: Blackwell Publications, 1996.
Koenigsberger, H.G. *Early Modern Europe 1500–1789*. Malden, MA: Addison-Wesley, 1987.
Roberts, John. *Penguin History of Europe*. New York: Penguin, 1996.
Sweetman, John. *Enlightenment and the Age of Revolution 1700–1850*. Malden, MA: Addison-Wesley, 1998.

## RUSSIA
Dukes, Paul. *A History of Russia c.882–1996*. Durham, NC: Duke University Press, 1998.
Freeze, Gregory (ed) *Russia: A History*. New York: Oxford University Press, 1997.
Hosking, Geoffrey. *Russia: People and Empire 1552–1917*. New York: Fontana, 1998.
Riasanovsky, Nicholas V. *A History of Russia*. 5th ed. New York: Oxford University Press, 1993.

## THE MUSLIM WORLD
McCarthy, Justin. *The Ottoman Turks: An Introductory History to 1923*. New York: Longman, 1997.
Robinson, Francis (ed.) *The Cambridge Illustrated History of the Islamic World*. Cambridge, MA: Cambridge University Press, 1998.
Wheatcroft, Andrew. *The Ottomans*. New York: Viking, 1994.

## CHINA
Blunden, Caroline and Elvin, Mark. *Cultural Atlas of China*. Rev. ed. New York: Facts on File, 1998.
Buckley Ebrey, Patricia *The Cambridge Illustrated History of China*. Cambridge, MA: Cambridge University Press, 1996.

## AFRICA
Thomas, Hugh. *The Slave Trade: the Story of the African Slave Trade 1440–1870*. New York: Simon and Shuster, 1997.

# INDEX

When using this index, please note that page numbers in *italics* refer to captions. Page numbers in **bold** type refer to the maps; the number and letter that follow give the grid reference. (For reasons of space, places are not indexed every time they appear on a map—if a map reference is given, it indicates that particular information concerning the place is shown there.) The modern country name is given in brackets.

# ACKNOWLEDGMENTS

**Front cover & 1** AKG; **2–3** Michael Holford; **6** ETA/Prado Madrid; **9** Bibliothèque Nationale; **10–11** Erich Lessing/AKG; **12** N.J. Saunders/Barbara Heller; **13 & 14** AKG; **15** Thomas Hoepker/Magnum Photos; **16** ETA/British Museum; **18–19** Dennis Stock/Magnum Photos; **19** Hulton Getty; **20 & 22** AKG; **22–23** Hulton Getty; **24** MEPL; **26t & 26b** AKG; **28** Erich Lessing/AKG; **29t & 29b** AKG; **32** ETA/Ironbridge Gorge Museum; **34–35 & 35** Erich Lessing/AKG; **36** ETA/Musée de Versailles; **38t** AKG; **38b** ETA/Decorative Arts Library, Paris; **38–39, 40 & 42** AKG; **42–43** Michael Holford; **43** ETA/Historical Museum, Moscow; **44** Michael Holford; **46** David Jacobs/Robert Harding Picture Library; **47** Michael Holford; **49** Images Colour Library; **50t** MEPL; **50b** Jeremy Horner/Hutchison Library; **50–51** WFA/Courtesy Christie's; **51** MEPL; **52** Bruno Barbey/Magnum Photos; **54–55** ETA/National Maritime Museum; **55** AKG; **57** ETA/Queen Victoria Museum; **58 & 58–59** AKG

**Timetable background** (5)15, 19, 23, 27, 31, 35, 39, 43, 47, 51 & 55
A map of the world by Gerhard Mercator, 1587 (detail): MEPL

**Abbreviations**
AKG    Archiv für Kunst und Geschichte
ETA    E.T. Archive
MEPL    Mary Evans Picture Library

**Artist**    Charles Raymond

*Every effort has been made to trace copyright holders of the pictures used in this book.*
*Anyone having claims to ownership not identified above is invited to contact Brown Reference Group plc.*